BUSINESS INFORMATION TECHNOLOGY SERIES

MANAGING THE HUMAN RESOURCE

BUSINESS INFORMATION TECHNOLOGY SERIES

Series Editor: TONY GUNTON

BUSINESS INFORMATION TECHNOLOGY SERIES

MANAGING THE HUMAN RESOURCE

John Westerman
Independent Consultant

Pauline Donoghue
Human Resource Manager, Digital Mobile Communications,
Wembley, England

Prentice Hall
New York   London   Toronto   Sydney   Tokyo

First published 1989 by
Prentice Hall International (UK) Ltd
66 Wood Lane End, Hemel Hempstead
Hertfordshire, HP2 4RG
A division of
Simon & Schuster International Group

Printed and bound in Great Britain by
BPCC Wheatons Ltd, Exeter

British Library Cataloguing in Publication Data

Westerman, John
    Managing the human resource.
    1. Personnel management
    I. Title II. Donoghue, Pauline III. Series
    658.3

    ISBN 0-13-547316-0
    ISBN 0-13-547324-1 (pbk)

Library of Congress Cataloging-in-Publication Data

Westerman, John.
        Managing the human resource/John Westerman and Pauline Donoghue.
        p.   cm. − (Business information technology series)
        Bibliography: p.
        Includes index.
        ISBN 0-13-547316-0
        1. Personnel management. 2. Manpower planning. 3. Office
practice − Automation. 4. Employees − Effect of technological
innovations on. 5. Information technology − Management.
I. Donoghue, Pauline. II. Title. III. Series.
HF5549.W4395 1989
658.3 − dc20   89-15941
                                                                          CIP

1 2 3 4 5   93 92 91 90 89

ISBN 0-13-547316-0
ISBN 0-13-547324-1 PBK

In memory of Ivy Dunnett and Raul Antonio E. Verde,
two colleagues who have gone ahead of us on the journey.

CONTENTS

Managers have asked repeatedly two key questions during the five years of our research for this book:

- How can they overcome inertia in their organizations?
- How can they develop a proactive approach to managing the human resources working in the ever expanding information technology environment?

In answering these questions, any suggestions we make must be able to solve a problem raised by the CEO of a large international group:

> Potential candidates for general management positions are not emerging from the computing function(s). Those candidates coming from the commercial areas, whilst having an understanding of basic computing, do not possess a comprehensive view of information technology, or appreciate the concept of information being a corporate asset.

In writing this book, our intention is to promote the development of comprehensive corporate strategies for the management of the human resources within the information technology environment(s) of the 1990s. We wish to encourage and assist managers (Chief Executive Officers, Personnel Managers and Human Resource specialists, Information Systems Managers, Technical Managers, and Support/liaison Managers) to confront the apocryphal claims for organizations of the last decade of the 20th century. Many companies are seeking technological solutions to these organizational challenges, but the criteria of earlier years has fuelled the impending pressures on human resources and there is a chronic shortage of appropriate skills in almost every area of commerce and industry, particularly within the information technology function(s).

Skills shortages have been the persistent backcloth when viewing the performance of information technology. It is likely that more failed projects, missed deadlines, and inappropriate systems are attributed to this single factor than any other. Managers, with direct responsibility for information technology or information systems, identify skills/staff shortages as a continuing (and perhaps readily accepted) element of the environment in which they work.

Many corporate executives with vision of the potential gain from the application of appropriate technology are angered by the apparent complacent acceptance of partial benefits, seeing that the full business advantage rarely is achieved – sometimes through lack of commitment or understanding.

We have been driven to writing this book because the constraining effect on change of inadequate strategies is so damaging in these times of the enterprise renaissance: times when the potential for business growth, success and benefit for national/international economies, is so great.

Frustrated by these long-standing problems, yet greatly encouraged by the growing emphasis on human resource management in many areas of corporate activity, we believe the time has never been more appropriate to face these problems head on in the information technology environment. We believe the skills shortages, as barriers to change, are only symptoms and not the underlying sickness.

We have looked at good and bad practices, success stories and expensive disasters. But the picture grows more encouraging as more organizations confront the fundamental HRM problems. Our book seeks to increase the success stories by encouraging those deterred by the frightening pace of change. The approaches we discuss are well proven management techniques for developing a culture where business and human benefits are achieved to the mutual gain.

The writers and the research team have a practical background and this has influenced our approach to the stimulating complexity of IT and HRM. We have endeavoured to take into account the day-to-day difficulties faced by corporate management.

Two detailed and extensive surveys were conducted to assist with the research background, and we had many discussions with executives from a wide variety of business and commercial sectors including: furniture manufacturing, high technology, advanced instrumentation manufacturing, life assurance, banking, retailing, paper manufacturing, book publishing, local government, pharmaceutical manufacturing, financial services, DIY and industrial tools manufacturing, regional health authorities, international airlines, and automotive products manufacturing. These research activities are described in more detail in Appendix 1.

Harrow and High Wycombe   Pauline Donoghue
January 1989   John Westerman

ACKNOWLEDGEMENTS

Many people have helped us to prepare this book, some directly, others unknowingly. In particular we acknowledge the professional support and friendly advice given by Stewart Segal, Bill Brant, Tim Ambler, John Cartwright, Iris Westerman, Ron Burgess, and Tony Gunton. We thank them for their searching questions and challenging stimulation.

During our review of the SIMA procedures, we much appreciated the guidance of Arthur F. Miller and Robert E. Gattorna – People Management Inc., Simsbury, Connecticut, USA.

Without the co-operation of all those managers who gave of their time to participate in the research surveys and discussions, we would have experienced major difficulties. Given the demands we made on their busy time schedules, we take this opportunity to thank them.

We apologize for subjecting Mike Cash of Prentice Hall to the nerve-racking experience of waiting for busy HRM and IT specialists to produce the final manuscript, and we thank him for his continued support during the process of giving birth to the book.

Finally, as we used computing facilities for our word processing needs, we would like to thank Ashley Poole, Laurie Lamb and James, who came to our aid with their technical advice and support.

CHAPTER 1

INTRODUCTION

Against a background of skill shortages and spiralling labour costs in most high technologies, why should Information Technology (IT) demand specific attention? We aim to convince our readers that managers have considerable control over the forces which cause the human resource problems.

It would be foolish and ill-informed to minimize the impact of human resource problems in the IT field. Businesses striving to maintain their competitive lead through strategic use of IT are frustrated in their endeavours as skills shortages extend project times and fuel escalating costs.

Most technologies have been developed over many years, with principles universally established, and supported by professional bodies. IT neither fits the chartered professional nor engineering moulds. It is more aligned to the activities of general management. The dilemma, a matter of perception and identity, allows information technology to grow in importance but without adequate management of the human resources.

Integration of IT career development with other management development programmes and practices is only found in a few top companies outside the major computer suppliers such as IBM and ICL. In the case of the latter two companies, IT is their business and not simply a supporting function.

Staff shortages have been an accepted condition throughout the history of commercial data processing. The acceptance accounts for the apparent inertia in managing the human resource. Could it be the 'mystery' of technology which prevents human resource management specialists becoming involved in this area?

Technical training is available from numerous sources employing the full range of learning techniques, as are induction and appreciation programmes. Why do some organizations spend freely on training whilst others refuse to invest in this way?

What is the motivation of those who work within IT? What are their inner needs? Are the needs understood?

Background

Throughout the history of information systems based on computer technology, from the late 1950s to the present day, the focus of management attention has been on hardware, software, project management, and individual applications. Human resource management in support of these activities has been limited to the recruitment and training of specialist personnel – but even these attempts by management have not avoided the acute shortages of information systems skills experienced by most companies.

Why are there so many human resource problems associated with the development of information systems? Is it possible to produce appropriate strategies, policies and action programmes which will create solutions to these problems? Will the increased usage of personal computers and the development of end-user systems solve or intensify these difficulties?

In addition to defining the problems, the key task of this book is to suggest a human resource management approach for overcoming the 'inertia syndrome' – how to facilitate the major changes required in corporate attitudes and policies which will allow for optimum contribution from information technology towards the commercial success of the enterprise. We wish to assist and encourage corporate management, faced with developing appropriate human resource strategies for the information systems environment of the 1990s. These managers include:

- Chief executives challenged by the need to implement changes in management style, or the establishment of innovative commercial approaches, both of which may be dependent on increased usage of information systems.
- Information systems managers, technical managers, support/liaison managers and staff, all of whom are having to re-orientate themselves to a corporate computing world which has irreversibly changed.
- Personnel managers and human resource management specialists attempting to assess and monitor the numbers of staff required to support these organizational changes, faced with understanding how end-users and information technology staff go about getting things

done, including their motivation patterns, exploring how employees deal with the stress and strain associated with computer usage, and how technical and social skills should be developed in response to the challenges of information technology.

- End-users confronted by the problems of taking on responsibility for and control of their own information systems, together with the need to understand the complexity of the people problems associated with increased computer usage.

The challenges for management

In addition to the many problems associated with maintaining traditional central mainframe and distributed computing, the emergence of end-user systems, exemplified by a rash of personal computers on company desktops, brings increasing challenges for those corporate executives responsible for developing commercial, information systems and human resource management policies. As suggested by Tony Gunton in his book *End User Focus*:

> Some organizations take an extremist view of end-user systems, and those which do so represent opposing extremes. On the left wing, there are those who see end-user systems as inherently good, and dismiss warning noises from the computer specialists as reactionary and self-serving. Those on the right see personal computers as a threat to the precarious order maintained by the systems department, and only permit them to enter with special permission (or, frequently, by the back door without it). In practice, however, there are no absolutes when it comes to controlling end-user systems, and these opposing extremes express the dilemma which has to be faced.[1]

End-user systems make major demands on the three main resources – information, technology and people. At the people/technology interface, the problem is how should end-users exploit the technology at their disposal? Whilst at the people/information interface, the problem is how should end-users access, manipulate and exchange information? These problems will require new types of managers and professionals. End-users and information systems specialists will need to adjust to new roles and develop additional skills.

Human resource management executives will be faced with increased pressures on manpower planning, performance evaluation, succession/career/education planning, skills analysis, motivational studies, salary administration, and recruitment policies.

The message to top management is clear. Whilst the technology burden will not diminish, it is vital to ensure that other aspects of management are given due attention:

- Integrating commercial and information systems strategic planning.

- Developing and implementing appropriate organizational changes.
- Implementing comprehensive human resource management policies.

End-user systems will require corporate executives to have a better understanding of organizational structures, the factors which motivate people, the design of work groups, the communication systems and processes (informal and formal), the building of methods to make more constructive the inevitable conflict between present and new organization structures.

Whilst we recognize the contribution end-user systems will make to improving the quality and service level of information technology, in this book we will not restrict our discussions to personnel working within this particular environment. The emergence of end-user systems places further pressure on managing IT human resources, but our intention is to review the human resourcing problems associated with all IT investments, be they central mainframe, distributed minicomputers, automated office networks, or end-user systems.

A way of viewing the people problems

When considering the management of the key resource – people – within the various information technology environments, it is useful to think of the problems encountered as being divided into three types:

- Problems which are about personal attitudes and motivation.
- Problems related to organization and task structure.
- Problems of developing and maintaining adequate numbers of human resources with appropriate IT skills.

We believe the solutions to these problems should not be developed independently, but should form an integrated approach which allows for the implementation of proactive corporate commercial strategies. The following chapters are about making things happen, rather than reacting to a range of dismal problems handed on from one management generation to another. We aim to provide readers with sufficient understanding of the basic problems, and enable them to develop a range of practical solutions.

Much general material has been written about human resource planning, people management, and information technology. However, there is a need to link together these topics in a format which will allow management to view the challenges and opportunities in a positive manner.

Certain authors have made major contributions which need to be mentioned:

- Douglas McGregor expounded the X and Y theory[2] in the early 1960s. Much of his insight is applicable to the problems of people management within the IT environment. How to build relationships which will lead to improved commitment to organizational objectives should be high on the priority list of all senior executives.
- The reported results of extensive research and counselling by Art Miller and Ralph T. Mattson[3] over the past twenty-seven years in Europe, South America and the USA, in the area of motivational patterning, will make a significant contribution to understanding the motivation and work attitudes of all those involved with the end-user systems environment. Given the challenges linked with changing roles for commercial and information systems personnel, the findings of Miller and Mattson suggest people cannot become anything they or others wish – they can only become what is in harmony with who they are designed to be. This has major implications for all managers responsible for education, training and people development.
- The writings and work of Professor Charles B. Handy[4] about organizational development have much to contribute to a better understanding of the difficulties associated with implementing successful end-user systems. Diagnostic abilities and skills in understanding organizations are all important. Diagnosis of oneself and one's own personal style of relating to people and organizations, diagnosis of others, their motivations, personalities and role problems, the varying factors which determine behaviour in groups and the differences between organizational forms, should all be included in management's thinking about successful strategies for any information systems environment.
- The work of Bennison and Carson[5] in the area of manpower planning has much to communicate to managers associated with locating and developing human resources for the information technology environment. The problems associated with manning an IT environment require a disciplined approach to establishing numbers of staff (supply and demand), the utilization of personnel, the development and education of employees, together with the construction of comprehensive human resource management policies, which not only respond to the immediate needs but which are the building blocks for the medium and longer-term corporate requirements.

References will be made, at various points in the following chapters, to the implications of these writers' findings.

There is a danger which should be avoided when discussing personal relationships, motivation, organizational development, and manpower planning, for the information technology environment. As with information technology itself, the technical considerations of managing people can absorb corporate thinkers to the extent that the reasons for applying the various approaches are lost in the mass of technical details. The complexities can lead executives and line management into forgetting the reasons why these activities were required in the first place. Whilst all these activities are necessary, management should ensure they place sufficient attention on careful identification and discussion of the basic questions and issues of the IT environment. The disciplinary need to concentrate on the issues requires the support of the Chief Executive and the corporate management team. Given that computer systems can be either a tool for assisting with the development of corporate commercial success, or an unpredictable time-bomb which can destroy management's best endeavours, the essential component – people – needs to be supported by appropriate strategies, policies and procedures which will lead to developing and maintaining adequate numbers of human resources with appropriate abilities and attitudes.

The key questions and how this book addresses them

What questions should be in the minds of corporate managers when thinking about information technology and the implications for the key resource – people? A starting list should include the following:

- What should we be doing about changing roles?
- How can we overcome the shortage of appropriate skills in the short term, and also build an adaptive base of required skills for the medium and longer term?
- What forms of skills forecasting should we be developing?
- How can we improve productivity within information systems during both development and implementation phases?
- How can we motivate personnel developing and working with information systems?
- Should we be using new training techniques (such as distance learning or knowledge-based systems)?
- How can we build effective linkages between corporate commercial planning, information systems planning and human resource management policies?
- How can we improve the quality of IT products/services and encourage better communication between information systems people and other parts of the organization?
- How can we retain skilled personnel and protect corporate investment in training?

These questions and many more are answered in the following chapters, and the checklists included in the appendices will assist readers to prepare audits of the situation in their own companies.

What are the various components of the problem? What should be the approach to the problems? These questions are examined and a schema defined in Chapter 2 which facilitates a deeper understanding of the relationships between human resource management, the IT environment, and the corporate culture.

Is there more to strategies than just planning? This question is explored in Chapter 3, highlighting some of the difficulties experienced by managers. Why should information technology make strategic planning more necessary? Why is integrated planning for IT rejected? What other activities are required? An examination is made of the commercial pressures placed on planning and human resource management policies for the information technology environment.

The opportunities and benefits offered by information technology raise a wide range of questions relating to the human resources. Where does the impetus for IT change originate? Why are there problems associated with changing jobs and roles for end-users and information technology specialists? What are the links between change, corporate culture, and the need for increased synergy? The strategic handling of change, and the human response to the challenges of the new IT environment, are discussed in Chapter 4.

Why are education, training and development of skilled people vital activities for the information technology environment? Effective provision of knowledge appropriate to corporate needs and individual career requirements will demand new approaches. What types of training programmes should be developed for the information technology environment? All these factors are reviewed in Chapter 5.

The emergence of end-user systems within the information technology environment will place stronger emphasis on personal characteristics and interpersonal style. Is it possible to motivate people working in the IT environment? What are the theories of motivation? How can theory be turned into practice? What are the real challenges? There are many implications for career choices – end-user systems technology and commercial demands prompt the need for new skills, abandonment of old skills and procedures, and the development of new organizational structures. These changes will involve much conflict. Management disagreements about principles often camouflage a collision of motivational patterns. Profiles of individuals which interrelate motivational pattern, the range of aptitudes possessed, and the attitude towards the new roles and opportunities will have to be developed. All these topics are discussed in Chapter 6.

Many companies are experiencing problems maintaining ageing systems based on mainframe computers. In addition, the emergence of PCs and end-user systems is revealing a hidden backlog of system requirements. Improving the utilization of human resources is of paramount importance, but measuring IT productivity is not easy. The work processes are complex and there is much debate about what should be the definable unit of output against which an input of IT manpower costs can be compared. Some approaches to measurement can mislead managers and they fall into the trap of concentrating on the detailed activities rather than the value added. Improved utilization will depend on companies implementing improved appraisal methods, restructuring work groups, understanding the connections between performance and job satisfaction, and using the IT productivity improvement tools which support the development and implementation of information systems. However, most of these tools are used by analysts and programmers. What evidence is there to suggest the tools can help end-users help themselves? All these aspects of improved utilization and increased productivity are explored in Chapter 7.

The most carefully conceived business objectives and corporate plans will fail if there are insufficient people with the right skills and abilities to carry them out at the appropriate time. This is very much the case with information technology. There have been occasions when important commercial projects have been abandoned, relocated or adapted significantly because IT labour requirements could not be met. Remedying shortages of other resources at short notice may be costly and embarrassing. Remedying an IT labour shortage, using contract staff or other external facilities, can be extremely expensive, and may at times be completely impossible within the timescales laid down. Manpower plans and human resource management policies which support information technology investments provide the essential framework within which it is possible to contain manpower costs and improve productivity. An approach by one company to effective manpower planning for the information technology environment is described in Chapter 8.

It is clear that the major issue in Human Resource Management for information technology is one of skills retention and development, against an apparently insatiable demand for these skills. The principal processes which make good HRM practice are known and accepted. Their application to the management of information technology staff appears problematic and discouraging. It is a common misconception that planning is impossible when the future is likely to change: the truth is the opposite. Lack of HRM planning in such situations has the potential for disaster. Chapter 9 examines the reality of the planning process, the practical procedures and policies necessary to maximize benefit for both organization and employee.

The appendices include a number of guidelines which can be used by readers to assess their investments in human resources within the existing information systems functions and those IT environments being developed for the final decade of the twentieth century.

Notes and references

1   Tony Gunton, *Business Information Technology: End User Focus* (Prentice Hall, 1988). Chapter 4 'Balancing toughness and tenderness', a comprehensive assessment of the problems and opportunities associated with end-user systems.
2   Douglas McGregor, *The Human Side of Enterprise* (Penguin Books, 1987).
3   Arthur F. Miller and Ralph T. Mattson, *The Truth About You* (Fleming H. Revell Company, 1977).
4   Charles B. Handy, *Understanding Organisations* (Penguin Books, 1983).
5   Malcolm Bennison and Jonathan Carson, *The Manpower Planning Handbook* (McGraw-Hill, 1984).

Further reading

Statement on Human Resource Planning (Institute of Personnel Management, 1986).
Strategic Relationships between Information Technology and Manpower Planning (Alliance Consulting Services, 1986).

CHAPTER 2
HRM PROBLEMS AND AN OVERALL APPROACH TO THE TASK

The HRM problem in IT is of such significance that it is clear a proactive approach must be employed. If progress is to be made by harnessing the power and competitive advantage offered by IT, the inertia and reactive response observed in so many organizations cannot be allowed to persist.

The proposition before us is no longer revolutionary: if we examine most organizational structures we find that they reflect the procedures, processes and manual systems of that organization. Take a textile mill – the development of the age-old spinning/weaving industry (a change which took a revolution to effect) was brought about by the coming of power from coal and engines.

Information, and the power of technology which allows us to exploit it, demands an equally radical approach to the organization. Database technology, structuring data from various sources, provides a greater value than the sum of its constituents. If implemented effectively, database allows for fundamental changes to organizational structure, which in turn has major implications for the associated human resources.

The role of human resource management must be recognized and an openness engendered in this sphere of planning. An understanding of a structure which must be built to enable effective HRM is essential to this aim. The schema outlined in this chapter will function most effectively in an organization where the nature and value of information/data has been explored and established.

What is human resource management?

Readers need to understand our usage of the term 'human resource management' and the difference between it and 'management of people'.

Human resource management (HRM) is one of those phrases that creeps into business language without any clear or positive definition. To some it simply means personnel administration, to others people management. HRM also has overtones connected with human and industrial relations. It is in fact all of these, and more.

The term 'human resource management' is used to describe a wide range of procedures and techniques used by corporate management to process and analyse an organization's human resource needs under changing conditions and includes developing personnel policies appropriate to the longer-term effectiveness of the organization.[1]

We use 'people management', within the context of this book, to describe day-to-day personal relationships entered into by individuals during the course of carrying out their work.

The obvious challenge of HRM lies in the unique character of the resource to be harnessed. People, unlike any other resource, react in a most sensitive way to their environment – and not always as expected. As with other productive resources, it is not difficult with sound planning techniques and appropriate control, to measure productivity (against appropriate targets) and to check the quality of output. But, whereas with other resources this information may lead rapidly to the solution of difficulties, with the human resource it simply identifies whether or not there is a problem. The underlying cause, the human response, remains unsolved.

The rewards of effective HRM lie not only in improved performance but in many other directions as well, such as reduced staff turnover, the reputation of the company as a good employer and, not least, in the personal satisfaction obtained by management both altruistically and in terms of their contribution to the company's welfare.

Human resource management and information technology

One of the functions where HRM is likely to be neglected is information technology. Most IT functions started as relatively small units. The new technology was both difficult and exciting. Initially, a high starting value was attached to the jobs concerned. Small teams of dedicated people would work round the clock, without prompting a financial reward, in order to get their system 'up and running'.

Over a period of time, for no very good reason, a certain amount of alienation from other sectors of the business community crept in. IT staff reacted in many cases by developing a rather self-conscious professional pride. This has occurred to such an extent that they are often accused of being professional at the expense of company loyalty, unfairly so since the two conditions are not mutually exclusive.

In any event, IT functions have expanded considerably. Departments of fifty people are common, some run into hundreds and even thousands. It is now taken for granted that new systems will work and that production will proceed smoothly and regularly – given capable management. Inevitably the early status symbol has disappeared and bureaucratic controls have been imposed. But this means that the days when high motivation and work dedication could be taken for granted are gone. The younger generation of IT staff, as with their colleagues in other sectors of business, are affected by and respond much more to their environmental conditions.

Yet IT is still a highly volatile area in terms of technological development, and senior IT management spend a great deal of their time trying to get the technical environment right. This is encouraged by the fact that, in many organizations, the IT Manager is expected to be the source of all technical expertise, and top management criticism of IT performance is often misdirected towards its technical competence. The fact is, as IT audits often reveal, that the value of time spent on matters of technology is offset by the corresponding lack of time given to overall general management, of which HRM forms a vital and substantial part. This often results in failure to deliver new systems on time, unplanned resource demands, gaps in the required mix of skills, and weaknesses in user communications.[2]

A great deal of attention has been given over the years to the technical problems of computing hardware and software. Large-scale digital communications networks, at international, national and local level, have been and are being implemented to support the needs of the next decade. Computer facilities have been brought into the office environment, not only by the on-line terminals to mainframe computers housed at corporate headquarters, but more so by the large numbers of standalone personal computers which are used to support word processing, spreadsheet and local database requirements. Earlier attempts to introduce an integrated approach to information systems have failed, and many of the manufacturing and supplying organizations have overstated the capabilities of their hardware and software to support the advanced concepts. The human resource has not been given due consideration, either in terms of the effects on end-user personnel of the automated processes themselves, or the needs for developing human resource management strategies and policies to support the manning requirements for the immediate, medium and longer terms.

For many commercial and information systems managers, the

concepts of human resource management, which include manpower planning, are seen to be activities which take place at corporate head-quarters. These corporate-level activities often result in broad generalized statements being made about people problems and manning levels – statements which are too remote from the actual problems faced by local management.

Our research findings suggest most companies do not attempt comprehensive human resource management to support their investments in information technology.

On the other hand, the complexities of forecasting techniques, establishing procedures for acquiring data, implementing productivity assessment systems, understanding motivational patterns, creating management development programmes, setting up skills inventories, and ensuring that all the modules are integrated correctly, can lead executive and line management into forgetting the reasons why these activities were required in the first place. Whilst all these components are necessary for a systematic approach to developing human resources, managers should ensure they place sufficient attention on careful identification and discussion of the local issues associated with information technology – especially with the advent of end-user systems.

How then should management approach the problems

A disciplined approach

As we explain in this chapter, human resource problems associated with the information technology environment require a disciplined approach to establishing:

* The numbers of people (supply and demand) required to develop, implement and run computer-based systems.
* The utilization of people, both technical specialists and end-users.
* The development and education of the key resource – people.

The resulting strategies and policies are required not only to respond to the immediate needs, but are the building blocks for medium and longer-term corporate success with information systems.

Evaluating performance and improving jobs

Performance evaluation and job design are of increasing importance in the information technology environment. Staff with information technology skills are to be found in many areas of a company, not just in the central computing function. The Office Technology Research Group recently conducted a study of information systems resource utilization by companies in the USA and Europe.[3] The report suggested there are problems in the following areas:

- Training and education of end-users.
- Staffing policies for the functions which help end-users to help themselves (where do and should these support personnel come from, and what career paths are open to them?).
- Managing the migration of these support personnel through a three-stage evolutionary process (missionary, business centre to planning unit or dissolution).

The function which helps end-users to help themselves is called an 'Information Centre' (IC). Its human resources originate in many cases from the central information systems function. In some companies, the IC consists of a mixture of technical staff and commercial personnel. If they perform their tasks efficiently and effectively, they will work themselves out of their jobs. The message for management is that an IC should be self-liquidating and build new skills in end-users.

Even without IC professional support, many end-users are developing a variety of information systems skills. These skills and their contribution within the commercial environment need to be evaluated, and where necessary the structure of work activities modified to gain even greater corporate benefits from information systems. Hence the need for performance evaluation and job restructuring.

Corporate response is weak and fragmented

The research studies for this book included two surveys of several hundred UK companies and detailed discussions with managers in forty of the organizations. Our research not only identified shortages of appropriate information technology skills, but also noted the paucity of performance evaluation and job design taking place within many companies. Few companies are running adequate performance evaluation of all personnel associated with information technology.

Of the 250 companies in our sample:

- One-third confirmed the performance of information technology personnel is evaluated and appraised.
- One-third stated that the information technology content of end-user jobs is not evaluated or appraised.
- One-third do not operate any form of performance appraisal system in their organizations.

In those companies where performance evaluation and job design take place, there are many different forms of techniques used. Some are operating procedures based on the 'Management by Objectives' (MBO) approach, others use a combination of testing and interviewing. A small number are attempting to develop procedures for evaluating the information technology element by appraising the attitudes of the individual and their work preferences, in turn linking these results to analysis of achievements.

Job design develops a better understanding of human needs

The term 'job design', when used in connection with the information technology environment, refers to the activities necessary for developing a better understanding of the human resource needs which will lead to more effective and efficient performance. The objectives of these activities are:

- To avoid deterioration of the information technology working environment.
- To avoid the building up of dissatisfaction and negative tension in relationships.
- To avoid frustration and friction at any level within the information technology environment.

To meet these objectives management must develop an approach, specifically for the information technology environment, which should include:

- The assessment of existing behavioural motivators and demotivators.
- The assessment of existing environmental factors which influence the performance of personnel.
- The building of a 'culture' in which personnel are given every encouragement to grow, where this encouragement can generate creative drive directed towards taking the corporate commercial and information technology strategic plans along in a positive way.

Management should be more concerned about measuring the return

We found corporate executives (commercial, personnel, and information technology) very guarded in their responses about the return achieved on the investment in human resources within the information technology areas of their companies. Many of the managers felt the approach of human asset accounting was not sufficiently well developed to be of practical benefit to their organizations. However, Paul A. Strassmann, former Vice-President of Information Products Group at the Xerox Corporation, makes the following important points:

We need to revise present accounting practices and taxation laws which recognize only traditional economic goods – land, buildings, and machines – as assets. Accounting practices do not recognize that human assets are the most important possession of any organization. In my view the value of the human capital of an organization is approximated by what is left after the 'shareholder equity' reported on the balance sheet is adjusted for expected shareholder returns on capital.

The conventional financial statement may dwell at great length on a firm's equipment depreciation practices without recognizing that people depreciate unless their work is replenished through continuous training, team work, motivation, and strong sense of belonging. The conventional corporate financial statement treats buildings as an asset and people as an expense. The opposite should apply. People are the only real asset and the building in which they work nothing but an expense.[4]

Although the total labour costs of information technology specialists are known in most companies, there is far less detail available about human resource costs for all personnel working with information systems. Often, the continuing financial benefits achieved by information technology are not known in sufficient detail. Apart from cost/benefit analysis during the original development of a project and an immediate post-implementation review, we noted very few companies attempting to maintain a continuous monitoring of the cost/benefits in each application area.

Clearly, corporate management should be more concerned about measuring the payoff from information technology in their organizations, including the investment in human resources. Not only is the current level of investment important, but the medium and longer-term commitments together with their implications need to be understood in much more detail.

Planning succession, career education and training

Human resource development seen in too narrow terms

Attention needs to be directed towards the development of all personnel associated with information technology – specialists and end-users.

The results of our research activities for this book suggest that, of the 250 companies included in the sample:

- One-third have coordinated manpower development plans.
- One-half admit to individual managers operating plans from the 'seat of their pants'.
- One-sixth operate no form of manpower development plans.

In discussion with several of these companies, we noted that end-users are not seen as part of the IT manpower development requirement. There is some reluctance to consider the growing numbers of personnel associated with end-user systems – who possess experience in word processing, spreadsheet, database, computer graphics, communications and electronic mail – as part of the manpower development requirement which supports the corporate information technology investment.

Information technology staff are seen as a world apart

Corporate management often referred to information technology personnel as 'special cases'. The same managers, when asked to define their classification of information technology personnel, were found to be restricting their understanding of the term 'information technology' to the central mainframe computer departments with their technical specialist staff.

An attitude exists, shared by many corporate commercial managers and central information technology personnel, that 'once an information technology specialist, always an information technology specialist'. It appears this is caused by a combination of corporate commercial management's perception of IT personnel, lack of opportunities for management development, and in many cases the fierce professionalism of computer specialists themselves.

The migration levels of IT personnel to the commercial areas, and vice versa, within companies included in our sample were very low. Given that the information systems skills barriers are being demolished between technical specialists and the growing numbers of experienced end-users (due to the increased usage of personal computers), the concept of 'the special cases' will need to be revised. Either there will be an increase in the number of special cases, or corporate management will have to change their perception of personnel working with information technology.

End-user training problems can be greatly alleviated in those companies where an Information Centre exists. But as a human resource development specialist comments:

...unless the Information Centre staff has had experience and training in course development and instruction, they may not be right for the end-user training job.

Training is a profession requiring unique skills and expertise. You wouldn't expect a high-school teacher to develop and program a payroll system if he or she didn't have experience and training in DP. Yet, often the Information Centre staff is expected to develop and teach courses without any experience in course development and instruction. Knowing how to use a software package and teaching others how to use it are worlds apart.[5]

The question is, *who trains the trainers?* Corporate management needs to make a positive response to this urgent problem.

Corporate attitudes typified by complacency and ignorance

Recent research conducted by a combination of government agencies and professional specialists in the UK suggests there is an unfortunately high level of complacency towards management development and training within British companies.[6] In particular the Manpower Services Commission and the National Economic Development Office firmly believe Britain's future international competitiveness and economic performance will be significantly influenced by the speed with which substantial improvements can be made in the scale and effectiveness of training by British companies.

The research findings of these government agencies suggest the level of complacency is reinforced by a widespread ignorance among top management of how their company's performance in training compared with that of their competitors – even those in the UK, let alone overseas. Furthermore, a surprisingly high proportion of the senior executives interviewed had only a limited knowledge of the scale of resources devoted to training within their own company.

Our own research investigations confirm the government agencies' findings. In many companies the training requirements for the information technology environment are either inadequately financed or subject to major cutbacks. Although there are examples of computer-based training schemes, these are not used extensively. Education and development activities are all too often either based on leaving staff to find out from fellow employees the best way to approach a particular problem, or alternatively personnel are being allocated personal computers together with some documentation plus floppy disk and told to get on with it. In the latter case, many packages are badly documented and the structure of the training techniques has received little attention from corporate management.

Underlying problems are no reason to avoid action

Several managers included in our research sample state they feel money spent on training within the information technology environment is a bad investment. This view is based on the high labour turnover of IT specialists, and with scant regard for the requirements of end-user personnel. These same managers have not given a great deal of thought to the costs associated with recruiting scarce replacement staff from the external labour markets, or the financial penalties and delays experienced during the interregnum. Clearly, these problems will increase as the pace of systems development accelerates.

There is an urgent need for many corporate managers to re-think their approach to the development of personnel associated with IT. The future success of commercial enterprises will be linked to the way in which they utilize information technology. Much of this success will depend heavily on the quality of personnel throughout the organization who must possess the appropriate skills. Management must commit themselves to developing human resource management strategies which include:

- Analysing the potential of its IT personnel (specialists, support staff and end-users).
- Planning their future careers to make maximum use of this potential.
- Providing the educational opportunities to develop the potential, and training personnel to work in the 'changed' corporate situations of the future.

Making the most of available skills

Skills analysis has too low a priority

Our research indicates that most companies give information systems skills analysis a low priority. Results for 250 companies suggest:

- Three-quarters have no form of analysis of IT skills (used or unused) performed.
- One-quarter maintain general files of unused IT skills within their companies.

Comprehensive skills inventories are rarely provided to support managers faced with developing human resource policies for the IT environment. Where inventories exist, the quality of information is variable. The data has a chance of being correct when an employee joins the organization, but the quality of this data deteriorates rapidly as time passes.

Many people have serious experience of home computers – not simply used for games – and this experience can be a valuable foundation for developing personnel required for the IT environment. Not one organization in our research sample was able to state they had conducted an internal survey of their management and employees to ascertain who had installed a home computer, and what type of experience this had provided for them. With the introduction of the Amstrad PC and PCW ranges, many homes contain professional business computers, and their owners have become quite proficient with a wide range of word processing, spreadsheet, database and communications packages. This experience will include having to overcome many of the problems faced by companies when attempting to introduce information technology into the office environment.

Where skills inventories exist they consist of details about foreign language abilities, certain technical skills (often only those used in the current job), professional qualifications (where these influence the remuneration of the employee), and experience in industrial/commercial areas within the current employer's organization. We found very few examples of skills inventories which include the experience gained by each employee throughout their career prior to joining a company. This latter type of information may have been hidden away in personnel application forms in deep store, but it did not appear to be available for quick access.

The skills inventories, for personnel working in the central IT departments, were in most cases known only to the local manager or supervisor. No companies maintained detailed records of skills available, used and unused, in the IT environment (central mainframes, distributed minicomputers, or dispersed personal computers installed with end-users). The skills inventories appeared fragmented with no attempt to integrate the information for corporate usage.

The advent of computerized personnel information systems (CPIS) may lead to an improvement in the situation, but only if managers perceive the need for this aspect of human resource planning.

Motivational study is widely misunderstood

Our research sample indicates that little usage is made of motivational study:

- Nine-tenths do not operate motivational studies of personnel associated with IT.
- One-tenth do not understand the term 'motivational studies'.

The term 'motivational studies', when used in the context of the IT environment, can be defined as a combination of:

- Identifying the basic motivational patterns, aptitudes and attitudes.
- Analysing the general and individual reward structures.
- Developing competitive payment schemes.
- Creating common fringe benefits.
- Monitoring the quality of working conditions.
- Controlling the organizational 'climate'.
- Nurturing the appropriate leadership qualities.
- Linking the direct incentives and output rates achieved.
- Implementing incentive methodologies.
- Ensuring an acceptable level of personnel involvement.
- Reviewing the possibilities for job enrichment via improved job design.

Many corporate executives misunderstand motivational studies.

Studies of this type are often greeted with a level of cynicism and distrust when linked to the challenges of the IT environment. Maybe this is due to management not being able to cope with several unknowns at one time – the uncertainty contained within the medium and long-term future for many companies, together with the theories of Maslow, McClelland, McGregor, Herzberg, and the work of Miller and Mattson, relating to human motivation.

More management education is required in this area of human resource management strategy.

Remuneration moves up the management agenda

Our research uncovered some surprises in the area of remuneration rates:

- Two-thirds state they operate rates based on standards for their industry or commercial sectors.
- One-quarter confirmed personnel remuneration for the IT environment is linked to local IT labour market rates.
- One-twelfth stated remuneration was geared to the national IT labour market conditions.

We had expected that the results would have been more heavily distributed between the second and third options – remuneration policies being influenced by local conditions, combined with national rates in a free labour market for scarce IT personnel.

A review of IT salaries over a three-year period suggests these are moving ahead far in excess of the local inflation levels. One-third of companies in our sample are setting the pace, whilst two-thirds are experiencing increasing difficulties when attempting to introduce flexibility into their bargaining situations.

The expansion of the IT environment will place the problem of remuneration higher on the list of management priorities.

Corporate management must understand the connections

End-users who are gaining meaningful experience with IT are beginning to ask questions about their own level of remuneration in relation to the salaries being demanded and paid to many computer specialists within the same companies. Corporate executives often feel that end-users are end-users, and that is the end of the problem. However, refusal to look at the problem does not make the problem go away. Increasingly, end-users are being helped to help themselves as a deliberate corporate policy. Central computer departments are still dealing with a backlog of demands for new systems whilst trying to maintain existing applications which have been developed over the years. The stresses and strains on central computing personnel, and the demands for faster development of commercial support applications, all lead to more rather than less end-user systems. The demand for mainframe computers is directly related to replacements for existing machines, rather than extending the number of central configurations. The growth is in national and local area communication networks, workstations, personal computers, word processing, spreadsheets, database, computer graphics, electronic mail and integrated office automation. Much of this growth involves the end-users in greater technical detail not only during the design and implementation phases, but at the later stage of keeping the systems up and going. End-users are moving out of the 'button-pushers' classification, and becoming skilled information systems practitioners. As such they are beginning to ask questions about remuneration.

Corporate executives responsible for human resource development policies in the IT environment will need to give much greater attention to this particular problem.

Recruiting information technology personnel

Recruitment is a chronic problem

Most companies have IT recruitment problems. Our research sample suggests that nine-tenths have major difficulties locating personnel to support their IT needs.

Recruitment of personnel from the external labour markets is proving to be a continuing problem for the majority of companies. We analysed the methods used by companies in our sample to match the demand for and supply of personnel in the information systems environment:

- One-twelfth forecast with precision their requirements for personnel.
- Two-thirds have a general understanding of their requirements for personnel.
- One-quarter make no attempt to forecast their requirements.

The recruitment problem is a combination of inadequate forecasting of requirements for IT personnel (technical specialists, support staff, and end-users), lack of investment in training, and too many companies chasing too few quality candidates. The increase in the number of recruitment consultancies and agencies indicates money is to be made from search, selection and contracting assignments, but client companies are still not finding IT personnel of the calibre required.

There are no straightforward solutions

After detailed discussions with several of the companies with no IT recruitment problems, we have to report that there is no one policy which can be singled out as the key to success. Companies in the financial sector are prepared to pay high salaries and offer a variety of fringe benefits. International airlines can offer a challenging technical environment, together with exciting fringe benefits. Some of the smaller companies have developed a corporate culture and human resource management strategies which make IT recruitment less difficult.

One company has an interesting range of applications, returns a good financial performance, and experiences no problem with recruitment. We were told the lack of labour turnover was undermining policies aimed at introducing new blood into the IT function. Their IT personnel are highly motivated, and appreciate the corporate culture. However, the company does not transfer IT personnel to other areas of the organization on a regular basis, and this policy has created a difficulty for them.

Many executives have a general understanding of their needs for IT personnel, but they simply extrapolate the demand and supply figures from the current situation. The medium and longer-term commercial demands of their companies are not being taken into account. Their analyses of why staff either stay on or leave the organizations are superficial. There are very few executives attempting to develop comprehensive human resource management strategies and policies for the IT environment which would lead to an improvement in the manning situation.

Shortages can be alleviated

Although there are shortages of skilled IT personnel, companies are not improving the situation by their failure to develop adequate training schemes. In addition there is no concerted effort to create procedures which will allow a planned recruitment approach for personnel needed to support the present and future demands for effective use of information technology.

The human resource management schema

This chapter has focused on problem areas within the information systems environment which require an effective and efficient approach to human resource management if they are to be solved:

• Identifying the supply and demand levels for IT personnel (specialists and end-users).

- Building skills inventories and making the most of available skills.
- Evaluating performance and improving jobs.
- Planning succession, career, education and training.
- Harnessing motivation, attitudes and aptitudes.
- Developing of appropriate reward structures.
- Recruiting IT personnel.

There is a need for a systematic approach to planning and monitoring people problems in the continually expanding IT environment. Problems within these areas can only be overcome by a comprehensive approach to human resource management. Managers must not make the mistake of thinking there are a series of simple solutions – there is no 'quick technical fix' available which will answer all the difficulties. Solutions to these problems are not a once-off operation, they require continuous attention.

The purpose of the schema

This is not an academic book about manpower planning – there are many excellent publications on the subject.[7] Instead we wish to direct the attention of readers to the management implications of people problems brought to light by this form of approach to human resource planning.

The schema, shown in Figure 2.1, provides ways of sharpening the focus and viewing the various relationships between human resource management and the IT environment:

- The inner circle identifies the procedures and policies linked with planning and monitoring IT manpower.
- The outer circle highlights the activities required to establish a corporate culture in which effective management of the IT human resources is possible.

Identifying stages of development

Companies are at different stages in developing human resource management strategies, policies and procedures for the IT environment. Some companies will operate many of the modules shown in the schema, others may be on the way towards building an integrated approach to human resource management for the IT environment. There are companies who are not aware of the need to begin identifying the problems and issues which have to be faced by corporate executives responsible for commercial, human resource management, and IT policies.

The schema allows executive management to identify where their own companies are placed in the development cycle of human resource management for the IT environment.

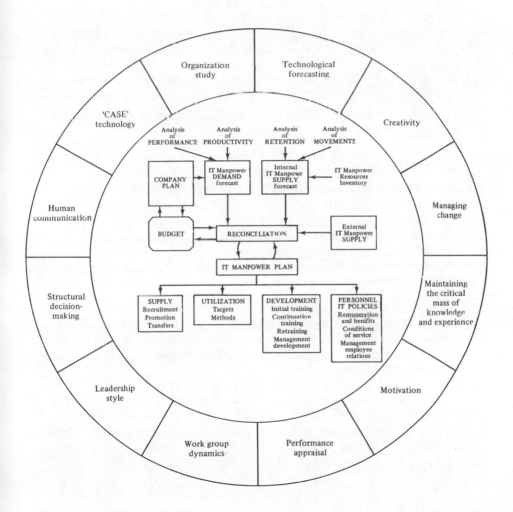

**Figure 2.1 A schema showing the relationships
between HRM and the IT environment**

The schema and the following chapters of this book

This book is not an installation manual for the schema. It is concerned with helping its readers to understand:

- The need for integrated planning of human resource management, IT and commercial requirements.
- The changing roles and shortages of IT skills.
- The demands for new training techniques.
- The motivation of personnel developing and working with IT.
- The implications of productivity tools for human resource management policies.
- The retention of personnel and forecasting of new IT skills requirements.
- The implementation challenges of this approach to human resource management for the IT environment.

The following chapters will discuss the areas identified in the schema, and assist readers to prepare a robust approach to human resource management for the IT environment of the 1990s.

Notes, references and further reading

1   *Statement on Human Resource Planning* (Institute of Personnel Management, 1986).
2   *Strategic Relationships Between Information Technology and Manpower Planning* (Alliance Consulting Services, 1986).
3   *What is an Information Centre and What Makes it Succeed?* (Office Technology Research Group, 1985).
4   Paul A. Strassmann, *Information Payoff – the Transformation of Work in the Electronic Age* (Macmillan, 1985).
5   Susan M. Boyd, 'Training's triumphs', *Impact: Office Automation*, 1985.
6   Several Government agency reports provide further information: *The Impact of Advanced Information Systems – the Effect on Job Content and Job Boundaries* (National Economic Development Office, 1983); *Investing in People – Management Training and Development* (Manpower Services Commission, 1986); IT Skills Shortages Committee reports (Department of Trade and Industry, 1984, 1985, 1986); *New technology and the demand for skills* (Manpower Services Commission, 1984); *Retraining for electronic skills* (National Economic Development Office, 1985).
7   The following books give extensive details on the subject of manpower planning: D. J. Bartholemew, *Manpower Planning* (Penguin, 1976); D. J. Bell, *Planning Corporate Manpower* (Longman, 1974); M. Bennison and J. Carson, *The Manpower Planning Handbook* (McGraw-Hill, 1983); C. Purkiss, *UK Case Studies on Forward-looking Manpower Planning* (IMS, 1981); C. Purkiss, *Corporate Manpower Planning in the UK* (IMS, 1981).

CHAPTER 3

IS THERE MORE TO STRATEGIES THAN JUST PLANNING?

We will be examining some of the objections to the planning of requirements for human resources in the IT environment and suggesting that none constitutes a sound reason why human resource management (HRM) for IT should not be as much part of the organization's business planning as other areas. If HRM is not already an integral part of the organization for IT, we promote the concept that it should be.

The emerging broader field of IT found in an end-user systems environment provides the scope for flexibility in planning human resources not practical in the narrower function of central mainframe computing.

We believe numerous problem situations common to many IT organizations have their root cause in the absence of comprehensive HRM, for example:

- The members of a prestigious project team, who have no idea of their longer-term future and who are forced to leave if they are to avoid stagnation or a maintenance role.
- The highly sought-after experts on one piece of software, who in a short space of time become experts in an antique software package, for which there is no Christie's!
- The valued loyal programmers condemned to support old, undocumented systems, while contractors work on the new glamour applications because nobody planned the manning aspects for the total lifecycle of the project.

- The excellent technician who cannot progress due to excessive earnings, resulting from unplanned salary strategies, such as the senior systems support specialist with an enormous shift allowance.
- The end-users who see the system as an electronic version of their former operation, who cannot take on board the fundamental conceptual difference between processes and the power of information technology, because nobody planned their education – a short burst of training when the system went live was inadequate.

The value of the HRM schema, already shown in Figure 2.1, needs to be understood and established so that it becomes a recognized and accepted process, interfacing with other planning processes.

The planning process, though structured, must be sensitive and flexible, capable of accommodating creativity in problem solving and not establishing insurmountable barriers or constraints for corporate management.

Background

Until the mid-1970s commercial computing applications were run either on mainframe equipment at corporate headquarters, or on external bureau computers. During this period much of management's attention was concerned with holding together the application development process. Priorities were recruiting analysts and programmers, wrestling with the emerging technology, overcoming the lack of proper working methods, procedures and disciplines, whilst at the same time attempting to control the costs.

In the second half of the 1970s many companies installed additional facilities, minicomputers, to process data at divisional or local functional level, with the summarized data being transported or transmitted to the central mainframe computers for corporate processing. These developments of distributed processing proved to be a rough ride for many companies. There were problems with the technology – incompatibility of mainframe and minicomputer hardware and software. There were many unresolved management control problems – battles about who should be responsible for the development, maintenance, and administration of the distributed data and application programs. The physical location of the development teams for these systems was argued fiercely. Many data processing managers fought hard to maintain control of short-term planning and operational control of distributed information systems.

Since the early 1980s personal computers have presented end-users with the possibility of developing, operating and maintaining their own applications. But many of the management disciplines established earlier by central computing functions are in danger of being undermined by end-users who have a natural enthusiasm for solving systems problems in their own way. Some companies have attempted to establish 'Information Centres' which help the end-users to help themselves, but which at the same time ensure there is appropriate quality control over application development.

Meanwhile, the central information technology functions have made progress with national and local area communications networks, which have led to a number of companies installing electronic mail, teleconferencing, and geographically dispersed databases. Applications can now be resident either on equipment controlled by end-users, or accessible from within the network environment – local or national.

Throughout the progress of computer-based information systems, planning has been increasingly dominated by the short-term project management approach. In the majority of companies, formal linkages between medium and longer-term information technology development, corporate strategic planning and human resource management policies, have not been established.

Information technology has made major advances in terms of reduced costs and increased power of hardware and software, whilst project management for individual applications has become more refined. But the disciplines of comprehensive strategic planning (including human resource management) have not made the same progress.

Why should information technology make strategic planning more necessary?

Paul A. Strassmann, former Vice-President of the Information Products Group at the Xerox Corporation, makes a very important point:

> The time required in the planning cycle for information technology strategies now exceeds that of the product planning cycle, the plant capacity planning cycle, and most likely also the research and development planning for almost every case I have examined. The time has come to take short-term, 'expedient', organizational politics out of the information technology planning cycle and incorporate it into the overall strategic planning discipline, since such planning is one of the longest lead-time investments an organization will have to make in managing its transition into the electronic age.[1]

Frequently, as consultants and practitioners, we are asked about planning by managers who have spent many years implementing information technology for their companies. When we enquire about the existing planning methods used, the replies remind us of either Lewis

Carroll's world of Alice in Wonderland, especially the King who said 'Begin at the beginning, and go on to the end; then stop', or Bertolt Brecht's comment in his play about Galileo, 'If there are obstacles, the shortest line between two points may be the crooked line.' In too many situations, the emphasis has been on short-term planning, ever more detailed project management, and the strengthening of information technology management's political will to survive the organizational changes suggested by technological developments. Rather than grasping hold of the opportunity to develop proactive approaches, reaction has set in and the 'inertia syndrome' has been strengthened. As suggested by McLean, Soden and Steiner:

> Because of the multi-year planning horizon of most computer-related projects, it is easy to equate long-range planning with any planning effort that has a horizon greater than one year. Thus fundamental questions such as 'Where is the information technology organization going?' and 'How is it contributing to the overall success of the enterprise?' become confused with 'What project should be started next?' and 'How can the continued development of existing projects be more effectively co-ordinated?[2]

In many organizations the planning methodologies for information technology are too simplistic and reflect only the local viewpoint of technical project management. The understandable concern for delivering systems on time and within the budget allocation can cause tunnel vision whereby management concentrates on project problems and technical difficulties. The planning problems associated with the emerging end-user systems are commented on by Tony Gunton:

> The performance of many information systems departments has indeed improved, but widespread dissatisfaction persists. Powerful new tools take time to perfect, of course, but the underlying problem is that management approaches are not evolving alongside the tools. The methods used to plan, develop and control information systems simply do not work for end-user systems. The skills needed by information systems specialists are changing, as indeed is the entire relationship of the information systems function with the rest of the business.[3]

The increasing number of business systems based on computer technology makes the development and implementation of comprehensive strategic planning methods of paramount importance. The planning methods used must bring together the commercial goals, the requirements for human resources, and the potential benefits to be achieved from the application of information technology.

Improvement in the quality of basic planning will lead to better short-term decision making, enhanced user communication, and a need for comprehensive human resource policies. In addition, a strategic approach to planning will allow better evaluation and ranking of opportunities for information technology, improved control over the requirements for human resources with appropriate skills, and optimized medium/long-term investment decisions. But success will depend on the quality of an organization's business planning, the performance of the information technology function, the criteria used to assess capital requirements, and how decisions are made about the needs for human resources.

Why is integrated planning for information technology rejected?

During our research activities for this book, an analysis of 250 companies in the UK produced the following results:

- Forty-four per cent claimed they systematically review and adapt their human resource policies for information technology personnel to meet the anticipated future demands.
- Twenty-two per cent operate highly integrated five-year strategic planning.
- Fifty-six per cent operate short-term one-year planning for budgetary control purposes only.
- Twenty-two per cent have no formal business planning!

The results suggest that seventy-eight per cent of the participating companies do not produce medium or long-term strategic plans, and yet forty-four per cent state they review and adapt their human resource policies for information technology to meet anticipated future demands.

We are left with the conclusion that many organizations are making their investment decisions for people, hardware and software, without due consideration of corporate medium and long-term quantified requirements – which we believe is a recipe for disaster.

Many corporate executives included in the research sample said they are unable to plan future requirements for human resources in their organizations. They define their problems to be a combination of:

- Uncertainty about the medium and long-term demand for company products due to increasing competition from organizations with production facilities overseas.
- Profit margins under extreme pressure.
- Bank interest rates continually changing.
- Shortage of appropriate technical skills in the labour market.
- Lack of adequate money in the corporate revenue budgets for education and manpower development activities.
- The financial institutions demanding inappropriate short-term profits to the detriment of medium and longer-term performance.

We do not believe these factors should be allowed to undermine the development of effective human resource management policies for the ever expanding IT environment. The problems have to be converted into opportunities, and if the problems cannot be resolved in their current format they must be redefined.

The challenges of overseas competition will not be answered by bemoaning the unfavourable comparison of labour costs. The need is for the development of more effective and efficient organization structures, supported by systems which make better usage of the associated human resources and allow for the production of high quality competitively priced commodities.

Narrow profit margins require highly sensitive control systems for supplies, inventory, production, distribution, and sales – for example, successful food retail companies have implemented sophisticated systems to monitor the effects of rapidly changing price structures which require fast feedback from electronic point of sale (EPOS) systems.

Continually fluctuating bank interest rates demand that companies have financial models, based on computing facilities, which forecast and update a range of corporate scenarios for planning in an age of continuous change.

IT skill shortages and competitors' poaching campaigns can be overcome by education and training programmes which support the medium and longer-term plans of individual companies. Retention strategies have to be developed, for IT personnel and end-users, and integrated with a wide range of other human resource management policies, all of which demand effective planning. Money for funding the development of IT personnel (specialists and end-users) will only be made available when managers take the opportunity to prove that investments of this type do pay off. We are convinced there is a more sympathetic view of education and training developing amongst commercial management, but the medium and longer-term benefits will still need to be quantified – all of which require detailed planning.

Answering the often unreasonable demands of the financial institutions, for short-term profits at the expense of the medium and longer terms, will necessitate the development of a commercial/personnel/IT management style which 'leads from the front'. Greater emphasis should be placed on a planning approach which counteracts all the negative factors given by some managers as reasons for 'throwing in the towel'. We recognize the challenges, but suggest corporate management should develop a range of proactive initiatives to neutralize the root causes of the difficulties rather than simply reacting or running for cover as each 'bomb' is dropped.

Yes, improved planning does assist, but are other supporting activities required?

With few exceptions, corporate strategies for effective information technology require a supporting framework of other management activities. The analysis of change, organizational study, technology forecasting, and the development of corporate cultures which allow for creativity, all have a major contribution to make in the building of comprehensive policies.

Understand the implications of technological change

Given that the great challenge of planning is to turn concept into action, the analysis of change is of primary importance. Unit increases in power and decreases in cost are fuelling the problems associated with technological change. We discuss change in depth in Chapter 4, but at this point it is worth noting some comments made by Christine Howarth in her book *The Way People Work – Job Satisfaction and the Challenge of Change*:

> However promising a change may look in theory, it will only work in practice if those doing the job are committed to making it work. All the evidence shows, that people are most likely to give their commitment to changes which they have themselves designed or influenced. Anybody else's change runs the risk of being seen as an imposed change and imposed change tends to arouse resentment rather than commitment. In practice there seem to be no short cuts. An organization needs the people who work for it to understand what they do, why they do it and how this relates to what others do. That sounds straightforward, but it is hard to accept and people have to learn from their own experience, not from others. They must be given time to have their own experience and find out for themselves. This understanding is too important to be confined to managers and specialists. The more widespread it is, the firmer the footing of the organization and the greater its capacity for responding to its customers. Since it is this capacity that will keep it in business, it is worth spending the time necessary to develop it.[4]

Often in our consulting activities, we have discovered that clients are spending a great deal of their time attempting to develop and implement complex IT strategies without giving due attention to the effects of major changes on their key investments – the human resources. The existing organizational structures of most companies are designed to achieve previous and current objectives – in no way are they geared to facilitating the development and implementation of radical changes. Any forward planning system for IT must be able to redirect the attention of management and end-users towards the new objectives. If medium and longer-term planning for IT is to be taken up by management, an openness to ideas and proposals has to be the accepted response – much easier said than done!

We discovered the following list, quoted in Vincent Nolan's book *Open to Change*, of sixteen ways to deal with new ideas. The list is of uncertain origin and cynical, but worthy of careful note:

How to deal with a new idea:

- Ignore it. Dead silence intimidates all but the most enthusiastic.
- See it coming and change the subject.
- Scorn it: 'You're joking of course', etc. Get your thrust in before the idea is fully explained or it may prove practicable after all.
- Laugh it off: 'Ho, ho, ho, that's a good one Joe. You must have sat up all night thinking that one up.' If he has, this makes it even funnier.
- Praise it to death. By the time you have expounded its merits for five minutes everyone else will hate it. The proposer will be wondering what is wrong with it himself.
- Mention that it has never been tried. If it is new this will be true.
- Oh, we've tried that before. Particularly effective if the originator is a newcomer. It makes him realize what an outsider he is.
- Find a competitive idea. This is a dangerous one unless you are experienced. You might still get left with an idea.
- Produce twenty good reasons why it won't work. The one good reason why it will is then lost.
- Modify it out of existence. This is elegant. You seem to be helping the idea along, just changing it a little here and there. By the time the originator wakes up, it is dead.
- Try to chip bits off it. If you fiddle with an idea long enough it may come to pieces.
- Make a personal attack on the originator. By the time he has recovered, he will have forgotten he had an idea.
- Score a technical knock-out; for instance refer to some obscure rule.
- Let a committee sit on the idea.
- Encourage the author to look for a better idea. Usually a discouraging quest. If he finds one start him looking for a better job.
- Accept it, but do nothing about it...it prevents the originator taking it to somebody else.[5]

As Vincent Nolan suggests, senior management too often attempt to create an environment in which the human resources feel they have to be right all the time. The safest way to do that is to stick to the known and the established, never to do anything new and different. But this is how an organization's arteries harden, imperceptibly, and the business continues to prosper for years, on the strength of past successes, until the momentum of the past begins to run down, and the company wakes up to a world that has changed around it. Desperately, it looks for new products, innovations of all kinds, but the innovative stream has run dry long ago; they have forgotten how to encourage and handle newness.

Many companies have an advanced state of 'functionalism' in their organizations. The arrival of new objectives which threaten to upset the established 'natural balance' of functions will be met with resistance. But effective information technology will necessitate major changes to existing functional structure, so understanding change and the way in which people react to it is an essential strategic component.

What about organizational study?

To manage change effectively requires management to mobilize its total resources in pursuit of the newly defined objectives. Developing an organization which can handle continuous change requires human resource management policies capable of supporting the appropriate basic processes, but more importantly the future management needs.

The results of our research activities suggest few companies are taking organizational study seriously. One-third of the participating companies admitted to detailed organizational studies being carried out by personnel management and information technology functions on a co-ordinated basis. Of the remaining two-thirds, half stated only the IT function is concerned about the impact of computer technology on job structure and future manning levels, whilst the remainder confessed no form of organizational study is being conducted.

There is much confusion between the broader issues of organizational study and the traditional organization and methods activities. We believe this is due to many companies concentrating on the short-term problems and giving little attention to the medium and longer-term demands. Organizational study does not rate highly on corporate priority lists – a dangerous situation for human resource management policies and the ever expanding information technology environment.

To say the human resource is the key to success and failure in the application of information technology, is a self-evident truth. People represent an investment from which an appropriate return is required. Managers and staff, as members of commercial organizations, also seek a satisfactory return in terms of economic and social needs. Failure to achieve the return, for the organizations, and managers or staff, may well ensure that commercial enterprises do not survive. Personnel perform their roles and tasks within an environment made up of structural and control components. The organizational culture, values, attitudes and behaviour originate from many sources, and are major contributors to the success or failure of companies.

Organizational study includes a wide range of activities in its portfolio:

- The understanding of different organizational structures and the factors to be taken into consideration when companies are faced with choosing a solution appropriate to their requirements.
- The improvement of personnel's perception and awareness of the commercial/industrial environment.
- The identification of factors which motivate people.
- The identification of corporate goals.
- The development of procedures which enable the goals to be achieved and monitored.

- The design of work groups.
- The analysis of leadership qualities, authority, power and influence.
- The building of methods to make more constructive the inevitable conflict existing within present and new organization structures.
- The increased understanding of the external environment in which the organization operates, and the information emanating from sources outside itself.

Much literature exists on the subject of organization theory. Researchers, writers, sociologists and psychologists, continually increase understanding of specific aspects of organization behaviour. But it is clear to us that although theories from any one area of study may be useful in helping management's understanding of organizational behaviour, single factor explanations are not likely to expose the complexities of real life.

There is a danger that too much of management's time can be given to analysing the internal processes within an organization, and too little given to the external environment. Some companies have detailed procedures for the flow of information on internal performance, but possess inadequate methods for gathering data and intelligence on the surroundings in which they operate. An examination should be made of the national/international macro-economies, legislative constraints, the position of competitors, the profit source of customers, technological trends, market trends, and market share.[6]

Several of the companies included in our research activities, which believe they have effective organizational study by personnel and IT management, were found to be viewing only the internal short-term implications of current information technology projects and not taking into account the medium and longer-term objectives. Whilst some commercial managers continue to say it is not possible to make plans in a time of uncertainty, many specialist managers directly concerned with developing human resource management policies for the IT environment are ignoring the external and longer-term realities.

Information technology, organization, and conflict seem to go together. Historically, there has been a great deal of conflict during the development of computing within most companies. Disagreement is bound to exist, but needs to be handled in a constructive manner. Inefficiency and ineffectiveness leading to conflict, may be used to describe minor procedural difficulties, or major commercial chaos caused by inadequate management control of IT developments. Senior executive management often consider these situations to be no more than a breakdown in line management's approach to 'government and control'. Line management receives the admonishment from senior executive level, and the government and control systems are tightened up in order to prevent a further occurrence of the deviant behaviour. If this approach to solving the difficulties becomes ingrained management behaviour, it is unlikely the real sources of the problem, other than the breakdown in management authority, will be identified and given appropriate attention.[7]

Professor Charles Handy argues that some key assumptions in organizational thinking have reached the end of their useful life.[8] They were only true up to a point, or for a time. We can no longer rely on them for the future. We need a new paradigm. Handy refers to T. B. Kuhn's book *The Structure of Scientific Revolutions*,[9] and states that paradigms seem to change when a new technology coincides with a shift in values or priorities – could it be that the new technology of micro-electronics will combine with a new value system to give us a new paradigm, a paradigm only awaiting its prophet?

Handy suggests at least four assumptions need reconsideration – all of which are significant to human resource management and information technology strategies:

- Economies of scale and specialization.
- Hierarchy is natural.
- Labour is a cost.
- Organization is a form of property.

Information technology demands specialists and breeds them. The concepts of economy of scale and specialization produced the tightly controlled IT organizations supporting the central mainframe computer functions. But as we now know, centralized information technology alone is not capable of continually delivering what the end-users require in a rapidly changing commercial environment. Far too many companies became, and remain, caught up in the program maintenance trap. Professor Handy believes, and we agree with him, that economies of scale (concentration) and specialization will self-destruct unless productivity increases always exceed inflation (i.e. the benefits of the formula exceed its cost) which has never happened in any industrialized country in recent history.

Specialization is another word for limitation. It can work effectively in IT organizations, but there are the dangers of boredom and alienation. The levels of sickness and absenteeism are danger indicators which need to be monitored carefully by human resource and IT management.

Does horizontal decision sequence need to be turned into a vertical ladder so that those who take the necessary earlier decisions are higher in the hierarchy than those who implement them? With the development of PCs and end-user systems, the decision-making process for information technology is reversed. Rather than having the high priests of IT making decisions for them, end-users are beginning to realize they can call the tune for which they are paying. But if this trend is allowed to develop in an uncontrolled way, there will be major troubles for end-users and IT specialists. We appreciate end-users do not enjoy being on the receiving end of bureaucratic decisions. But the advent of PCs has provided end-users with 'hijack power' (a term used by Professor Handy to describe those at the receiving end having negative power at least equal to the positive power of those at the other end). The emerging end-user systems will make us all rethink the approach to decision-making in the information technology environment.

IT human resources (specialists and end-users) are seen by far too many companies as being simply labour costs to be recorded in the profit and loss account. This has led to an unfortunate impact on how IT organizations are managed. Costs are items we attempt to minimize, and labour becomes alienated once it becomes figures and not individuals. We know of several companies who reduced their investments in IT human resources to counter the effects of short-term commercial pressures, only to find themselves facing major problems resourcing projects less than twelve months later. We recommend that IT human resources are seen as an asset to be disposed of only after careful thought has been given to its alternative uses.

The concept of who owns the organization is open to question. Given the demands by the financial institutions for ever higher short-term profits, at the expense of medium and longer-term investments, it can be argued that shareholders are providers of finance, with privileges proportionate to the risk they run, rather than owners. Does ownership have any real meaning? Professor Handy suggests that organization is beginning to be thought of as a community rather than a property, and the difference is more than semantic. Many different kinds of people have a stake in an organization – the customers, the employees, the financiers, and the government. The same can be said about Information Technology organization – systems are not owned by the technical specialists, but neither are they totally owned by the end-users. Many people have an interest in the strategic management of information. The concept of information being a corporate asset is gradually gathering strength, but the reactionary ideas of 'personal property' are a long time dying!

Why are we caught out by technological developments?

Despite all the work by various Information Technology research groups in Europe and the USA, many companies continue to be caught off guard with each new development in hardware and software, especially in terms of the impact they have on organization, the human resources, and existing project plans. We believe this is due to the lack of technological forecasting.

During our travels whilst researching for this book, we came across the following quotation from Dante's Divine Comedy. It was sited above the door to a manager's office (the manager was responsible for developing the information technology forward plans):

Per me si va nella citta dolente,	(This way for the sorrowful city,
Per me si va nell'eterno dolore,	This way for eternal suffering,
Per me si va tra la perduta gente ...	This way to join the lost people ...
Lasciate ogni speranza voi ch'entrate!	Abandon all hope, you who enter!)

Can the information technology forward planning environment be so fraught? Paraphrasing a comment made by Herman Kahn: the management of innovation and technological forecasting is not only concerned with future events, making the desirable more likely and the undesirable less likely. They try to put policy-makers in a position to deal with whatever future actually arises, to be able to alleviate the bad and exploit the good. Far from abandoning hope, this is where it may be found!

The rapid implementation of PCs by end-users from the early 1980s onwards has overturned many a medium- and long-term IT strategic plan produced in the previous decade. The arrival of mini-computers and distributed systems caused ripples of concern for some, and smiles of satisfaction for others. Converged communications and computer technology, supporting both voice and data transmission requirements on an integrated basis, caused major growth in the implementation of communications networks, but lack of agreed technical standards became apparent. Database management systems for mainframes were very slow to take off – many of the earlier implementations were technical and commercial disasters. But this approach to information management is gathering momentum with plans to implement databases operating across a mix of mainframes, minis, and personal computers, all linked by sophisticated communications networks. We can see the needs for agreement of data definition and usage standards becoming a management priority. Back in 1963 John Diebold said in an address to Columbia University:

> Today's crops of machines deal with the very core of human society, with information, its communication and use. These are developments that offer far more to mankind than net changes in manpower, more or less employment or new ways of doing old tasks. This is a technology which vastly extends the range of human capability, and which will fundamentally alter human society, and force us to reconsider our whole approach towards society and to life itself.[10]

Yet, over twenty-five years later, we see IT opportunities and benefits still being lost. Too many companies continue to think of information technology in terms of reducing manpower investments, and implementing increasingly more sophisticated and powerful new hardware/software to support old tasks.

When an organization is created to handle a long-term requirement, the one thing planners can be sure of is that conditions, pressures, and demands on the organization will change from time to time. The tempo of activity will change; so will the scale of operations. However, neither the timing nor the nature of the changes can be foreseen precisely. How are such uncertainties to be taken into account?

In technological forecasting an attempt is made to generate a listing of possibilities. By applying the best available information, analyses, and creative thinking, management hope to anticipate events. But like any other method of forecasting, technological forecasting can only be as accurate as the information fed into it – information from the past, knowledge about the present, together with our thought processes, insight and judgment.

A whole range of forecasting techniques exist, but they can be divided into two types: exploratory and normative. The exploratory category includes all those techniques which are based upon an extension of the past through the present and into the future, whilst normative methods start from the future, then trace backwards to determine the necessary steps required to reach the end point.

In practice it is necessary to employ a combination of techniques (trend extrapolation, precursor trend curve matching, substitution analysis, Delphi, technology monitoring, scenarios, relevance trees, and cross-impact analysis), some of which may be exploratory and some normative. Although technological forecasting is about generating a range of scenarios of the future, the temptation to put too much stress on making the future happen has to be avoided. To quote Peter Drucker:

> Decisions exist only in the present. The question that faces the long range planner is not what we should do tomorrow, it is: What do we have to do today to be ready for an uncertain tomorrow? The question is not what will happen in the future. It is what futuristics do we have to factor into our present thinking and doing; what time spans do we have to consider, and how do we converge them to a simultaneous decision in the present?[11]

Technological forecasting does not ensure that a decision maker predicts the future with positive certainty. The techniques assist in the refining of judgments. The success of the methods is totally dependent upon the quality of information made available and the quality of minds applied to it. We recommend serious consideration be given to using technological forecasting, but remember the techniques will never completely remove the uncertainties of the future.

Why stress the need for creativity?

We believe the effectiveness of 'human resource management' and 'managing the human resources', in the current and emerging IT environments, depends upon the quality of ideas. Creativity is the keyword. IT specialists, end-users, and commercial/personnel/IT managers must all generate an environment where new ideas can be freely discussed.

Why is it some organizations are better at generating new ideas, whilst others appear to stifle creativity? Are creativity and planning mutually destructive?

As Anthony Jay has said:

> Change is not a sideline in the business of leadership, it is integral to the whole idea: to describe a person as a great leader, who left things exactly as found, is a contradiction in terms. A leader may change the map of Europe, or the breakfast habits of a nation, or the capital structure of an engineering corporation: but changing things is central to leadership, and changing them before anyone else is creativeness.

During our research activities we found few companies actively promoting creativity as a desirable personal quality. Indeed, several managers suggested imagination and insight cause too many problems – 'We want doers not creative thinkers'. However, we continue to believe that creativity and its development should be high on the list of management priorities.

Those organizations which are better at generating new ideas for effective and efficient IT have developed a positive approach to creativity by:

- Ensuring appropriate creative ability exists at all levels (managers, specialists and end-users).
- Identifying the level of creative potential in each person.
- Analysing each job and determining the amount of creativity required to perform it effectively.
- Matching personal creative capabilities with the requirements of each job.
- Developing a working environment in which creative ideas are received in a positive manner, in which creative contributions to current projects are encouraged.

Imagination plays an important part in the act of being creative – invention is a non-rational process. We believe defining the strategic problem is where creativity is required, whilst developing solutions becomes a matter of identifying obvious steps. Sir James Taylor quotes an interesting historical case:

> Creativity is now, and always has been, inhibited by conventional wisdom and established habits. For example, the horse-drawn chariot, which included that fantastic invention, the wheel, was almost certainly used 4,000 or 5,000 years BC which was before anyone had the simple idea of riding the horse. A complicated solution of a problem often precedes a simple one.[12]

IT specialists and many end-users are 'potty-trained' not to allow their minds to wander, and self-imposed boundaries are considered to concentrate the mind. It is difficult to nurture creativity in such a situation, but the problems can be eased by establishing matrix-structured multi-disciplinary project teams. Team members are likely to come from quite different backgrounds, and new ideas can emerge providing management ensures everyone is motivated to present creative suggestions. Most thinking about IT is constrained by past experience and training. Management faced with new problems (opportunities) attempt to apply old solutions. As with normative methods for technological forecasting – where our minds are pushed forward to some point in the future, followed by finding the path back to the present – the development of creativity requires an escape route from traditional ways of thinking. This is more easily said than done!

Most of us tend towards rejecting new ideas. Edward de Bono[13] illustrates this human characteristic by showing a radical new design of a wheelbarrow to a group of people. His proposal has both merits and weaknesses, but the reactions of the group are almost invariably negative, concentrating on the failings of the design to the almost total exclusion of its advantages.

There are a wide range of analytical and non-analytical techniques for problem solving. The analytical methods are based on 'normal' logic processes, whilst the non-analytical methods are aimed at stimulating the imagination. But the real problem to overcome, when attempting to improve the level of creativity in an organization, is scepticism. Despite this difficulty, we believe organizations downgrading the creative personal quality are living on borrowed time.

Planning and human resource management

In this chapter we have explored the historical background to planning for IT, why strategic planning is increasingly more necessary, why medium and longer-term planning is rejected by some managers, and the need to consider our response to the challenges of change, technological forecasting, organizational study, and creativity.

Human resource management practitioners have a major contribution to make when providing effective support for information technology strategies. However, even with appropriate planning activities, success will be dependent on the attitudes of individual managers (commercial/personnel/IT) and the quality of the corporate culture. We agree fully with the comment made by Tony Gunton:

> Recently, a number of companies have been strikingly successful in finding innovative ways of applying information technology to achieve competitive advantage in their markets, and this has focused attention on methods for recognizing such opportunities. This search has been fuelled by new ways of looking at how businesses work, such as the value-chain concept developed by Michael Porter. Insights such as those which gave rise to the well-publicized successes are rare, and, judging by what we know of how they were achieved, seem to have been born more out of inspiration than out of systematic planning. Therefore, it is arguable how far the big

opportunities can be recognized by the formal planning process. Nonetheless, the prizes for success are considerable, and hence many companies are working hard to crack the problem.[14]

Notes and references

1 Paul A. Strassmann, *Information Payoff – the Transformation of Work in the Electronic Age* (MacMillan, 1985).
2 Aphraim R. McLean, John V. Soden and George A. Steiner, *Strategic Planning for MIS* (John Wiley, 1977).
3 Tony Gunton, *Business Information Technology: End User Focus* (Prentice Hall, 1988).
4 Christine Howarth, *The Way People Work – Job Satisfaction and the Challenge of Change* (Oxford University Press, 1984).
5 Vincent Nolan, *Open to Change* (MCB Publications Limited, 1981).
6 David J. Smalter, 'Organizing for change', in *Long Range Planning for Management* edited by David W. Ewing (Harper and Row, 1972).
7 P. Bryans and T. P. Cronin, *Organization Theory – the Study of Human Relations within the Business Organization* (Mitchell Beazley, 1983).
8 Charles B. Handy, *Understanding Organizations* (Penguin Books, 1981).
9 T. B. Kuhn, *The Structure of Scientific Revolutions* (University of Chicago Press, 1962).
10 David W. Ewing (editor), *Technological Change and Management* (Harvard University Press, 1970).
11 Peter F. Drucker, *Technology, Management and Society* (Heinemann, 1970).
12 Sir James Taylor, proceedings of conference *Luck, serendipity or planning* (The Research and Development Society, 1970).
13 Edward de Bono, *Lateral Thinking for Management* (McGraw-Hill, 1971), and *Practical Thinking* (Jonathan Cape, 1971).
14 Tony Gunton, *Business Information Technology: End User Focus* (Prentice Hall, 1988).

Further reading

H. Jones and B. C. Twiss, *Forecasting Technology for Planning Decisions* (Macmillan, 1978).
H. A. Linstone, and M. Turoff, *The Delphi Method: Techniques and Applications* (Addison-Wesley, 1975).
H. Sackman, *Delphi Critique* (Lexington Books, 1975).
J. P. Martino, *Technological Forecasting for Decision Making* (Elsevier, 1983).
H. Nystrom, *Creativity and Innovation* (John Wiley, 1979).
R. C. Parker, *The Management of Innovation* (John Wiley, 1982).

CHAPTER 4

CAN WE PREPARE FOR CHANGE?

True flexibility is a revolutionary quality, a capacity for fundamental change in working methods and approach, together with changes of values.

Over the years IT jobs have been created and terminated. Advances in technology, such as 4th Generation Languages and remote job entry, have relieved pressure on scarce skills in one area only to create new needs in another.

Changes in legislation and trading have influenced systems demanded by business leaders, and are reflected in the skills required of IT staff. For those who have been involved in resourcing IT teams over the years, it is clear how inflexible attitudes are to skills, and how conservative is the approach to resourcing.

Why are there problems with the changing jobs and roles of IT managers, specialists and end-users? The reasons include:

- Many of the new jobs and roles are not understood, yet managers classify them as sophisticated and make demands for precise and extensive experience.
- Broader management skills are not being developed early enough in the careers of IT professionals.
- Skills requirements are not specified realistically – there is evidence that many organizations over-recruit in terms of academic and technical requirements.
- Not enough attention is given to motivation and personal qualities – adaptability, social skills – which leads to a reduction in flexibility when attempting to resource the end-user systems environment.

- Elements of change are not always recognized – it is easy to identify with a change in a programming language or hardware environment, yet not always so easy when the change is gradual and subtle, but fundamental.
- Organizations are too slow responding to skill shortages, which leads to much time spent on exhausting, expensive, and often fruitless recruitment campaigns.
- IT functions create cultures which are maintained by careful self-perpetuation (cloning), resulting in rigidity and insensitivity to change.
- Too many managers are obsessed with the old sort of confrontation and threat regime, rather than co-operation and trust which represents tomorrow's businesses based on telecommuting.

Background

Change is a condition we experience in every aspect of our lives. Whether we welcome it or not, change rears its head at every turn. To exist is to enter into the process of change. As Tom Peters suggests:

> To meet the demands of the fast-changing competitive scene, we must simply learn to love change as much as we have hated it in the past....Every variable is up for grabs, and we are meeting (not meeting, in general) the challenge with inflexible factories, inflexible systems, inflexible front-line people – and, worst of all, inflexible managers who still yearn for a bygone era where presiding over the opening of new wings of hospitals and new plants was about the most strenuous chore to be performed.
>
> Today, loving change, tumult, even chaos is a prerequisite for survival, let alone success.[1]

In the area of information technology, the pace of change is accelerating. Technical specialists and end-users are expected, ever more frequently, to come to terms with new hardware and sophisticated software. The acceptable development and implementation timescales for IT projects are becoming shorter and shorter. Information systems are having to be developed which can adapt to sudden acquisition and divestment of product groups, subsidiary companies, or even total corporate mergers.

Information technology managers and technical specialists are sometimes called 'agents of change', but many of them will admit, in unguarded moments, that change is good for all end-users but not so welcome within the IT function itself. This attitude is likely to be linked with many years of investment in developing technical skills whilst implementing monolithic information systems based on mainframe computers. A similar attitude is developing amongst some end-users who have spent valuable time and effort developing their own systems on PCs, with or without the assistance of Information Centre staff. Managers who have attempted either to persuade secretarial personnel to move from one much loved word processing system to another, or to implement corporate policies for standardizing on specific spreadsheet packages, will recognize the situation. The very title of this chapter could give the impression that the implementation of IT can be a fully planned and comfortable experience. We recognize that the reality is quite different, and as Dr Johnson said 'Change is not made without inconvenience, even from worse to better'.

Whilst preparing for this book we reviewed attitudes towards change, especially within the IT environment. Our findings suggest that many IT managers, specialists and end-users, need to give more thought to what is understood and meant by the words 'success' and 'failure'. Unfortunately, change is thought of in terms of succeeding or failing. Clearly all changes involve risks, and nobody can know exactly how everything will work out. Those readers who have a science background recognize that scientific advances are made by adventurous experimenting, and that many of these activities do end in blind alleys. But, as stated in the previous chapter, senior management often attempt to create a commercial environment in which the human resources feel they have to be right all the time, and this can lead on to semi-official strategies for resisting change.

During the industrial revolution the concept of limiting liability was crucial to its success, and it could well be the same for the information technology revolution. The challenges of change for IT personnel (managers, specialists and end-users) imply risks, but how to limit the effects of the risks without reinforcing the status quo?

Those managers responsible for creating IT strategies will be expected to possess a firm understanding of the more difficult and disagreeable actions which will have to be taken if technology is to be implemented successfully. Human resource managers need to assess the demands for the development of new skills (resourced by retraining and/or external recruitment), examine the implications for early retirement or redundancy, and develop training plans for communicating the IT strategy to all levels of the organization.

In the UK, the forecast fall in the number of young people available for employment during the middle to late 1990s is cause for concern. Already, some companies are having difficulty recruiting staff with the necessary skill levels, and this situation will become more widespread unless employers respond positively to these changes. The increase in demand from industry and commerce for young people could well lead to some being attracted away from higher education, leading to a reduction in professionally qualified manpower in later years.

The Chief Executive Officer (CEO) must fully appreciate the costs (human and financial) which will have to be met if the organization is to enjoy the full benefits of change. Most management texts suggest plans for change cannot be implemented without the full support of the CEO. We appreciate the point being made, but the advice leaves us with the mental picture of the CEO sitting astride a white charger called 'change', giving rousing calls to action, and rushing into the fray whilst the rest of the organization looks on in relief, amusement or disbelief! The success of a major change in IT strategy, such as a substantial shift towards end-user systems, depends on changing attitudes and restructuring the work of existing managers, IT specialists, and end-users. Some of these will not find it easy to accept the changes in responsibility, or adapt to different management/work styles. It requires much skill to transform people, and gain their support for shaking the status quo.

The essence of successful change lies not so much in the detailed design of the plans, but in the abilities of managers, IT specialists, and end-users to alter their behaviour in line with the new principles which the changes seek to implement. Change is about altering behaviour, not revising organizational charts – if this is not appreciated, there can be no hope of gaining the full benefits offered by information technology.

Where does the impetus for change originate?

Should the impetus for change originate from a central planning group? Formal corporate planning began to be popular with large-scale companies during the late 1960s/early 1970s. Since then the function has passed through many phases:

- The initial step consisted of a part-time planning committee reporting to senior executive management. But the pressures of day-to-day work dominated the time of most committee members, so medium and longer-term planning activities tended to become less effective as time passed.
- The second phase consisted of appointing a full-time executive director to lead the function, and the secondment of individuals from line management to work on specific projects.
- The next phase saw the seconded staff being placed on a permanent basis within the corporate planning function.

The director of the function has to be in the mainstream of management thinking where it is possible to have continuous dialogue with the managers who are responsible for 'making things happen'. The standard textbooks on planning suggest the posture of a corporate planning specialist ranges from a passive attitude as counsellor or co-ordinator, to a forceful, dynamic stance as an initiator or entrepreneur who deals with the substance and execution of plans.[2]

But should the initiation and impetus for change be left to the corporate planning function? Responsibility for IT strategies and policies for human resources are often left with the specialist practitioners, sometimes deliberately, occasionally by default. What about the line managers and their staff – are they supposed just to 'drive the buses and halt only at the official stops' in accordance with the corporate planning/IT/HRM timetables? The answer to this question depends on whether organization is seen as a highly disciplined hierarchical structure or a community to which everyone belongs. We believe line functions, as with end-user systems, should fully enter into the process of making decisions about change. The planning of change should be seen as an integral part of line management's responsibilities. Where line management is committed to implementing change, the possibilities for success increase tremendously.

Andrew Leigh quotes the example of how, when John Welch became chairman of General Electric in the USA, the first thing he did was to dismantle the company's strategic planning department. Welch had reviewed the previous twenty years and discovered that each of GE's major internally grown business successes came from outside of the strategic planning system. Intensive research together with sophisticated planning processes are no panacea.[3]

Impetus for change originates from the free interaction of views and ideas. Organizations which give space for creativity will find that a positive response to change(s) goes in parallel with less concern for position and status. Flexible planning will be encouraged, and the possibility of everyone feeling motivated towards the objectives of change will be enhanced. Successful changes are based on adequate channels of communication which make it not only possible but probable that good ideas generated at any point within the organization reach those who can make good use of them.

Changes of job title or changes of role?

The process of implementing IT strategies, even in an environment where flexible planning and free interchange of ideas are part of the corporate culture, raises questions about the differences between job titles and roles. For example, company ABC has decided to implement multiple end-user systems, in addition to the existing mainframe computer facilities. The company's commercial, personnel and IT management recognize the need to develop a supporting function, an Information Centre, which has responsibility for helping the end-users help themselves. So far so good, but can members of the central mainframe installations be transferred to the new Information Centres without retraining? Do the new jobs require the incumbents to play new roles? The new positions will require the development of new job descriptions, but to what extent do the descriptions define the actual role to be played? How far have the personal qualities and behavioural elements of candidates been taken into account? Being a systems analyst for financial applications running on central computing facilities does not guarantee the person will be effective in the new situation of advising and guiding end-users to develop financial modelling applications on their own PCs. Some of the technical and application knowledge may be appropriate, but interacting with end-users in a totally different work group situation may well require the individual to play a behavioural role which is not within his or her nature. We would emphasize a move from one job to another is more than change of job title – the incumbent is faced with responding to a possible change of role.

To appreciate fully problems associated with changes of role, it is essential to understand a number of basic concepts. These are ambiguity, conflict, differentiation, expectation, and perception associated with performing a role within any organizational structure.

Role ambiguity

Employees associated with the evolving IT environment, managers, technical specialists, and end-users may be uncertain about key requirements of their jobs, and how they are expected to behave in them. This occurs when individuals are uncertain about the scope of their responsibilities and objectives, the limits of their authority, specific production requirements, and the criteria used in evaluating their work. Most people dislike such uncertainty, and find it stressful. In a research study conducted in the USA it was found that between thirty-five to sixty per cent of employees interviewed experienced ambiguity to some degree.[4] Such ambiguity will generate high levels of stress from the uncertainty and lead to below optimum performance.

Role conflict

People associated with developing and implementing information technology, like other areas of rapid change, experience a considerable degree of role conflict.[5] The conflicts are far from rare, because most people have several different roles to play, and must deal with groups of persons holding contrasting expectations about their behaviour both at work and in their private lives. For example, growing family commitments generate both positive and negative demands.[6]

There are two main types of role conflict: inter-role and intra-role.

Inter-role conflict refers to the incompatible demands of two or more different roles played by the same person – the problem of being the 'boss' and a 'friend', where it is difficult to fulfil the demands of both roles at the same time. In intra-role conflict, by contrast, there are contradictory demands within a single role as viewed by other members of the group – the problem of supervisors being expected to be loyal to their fellow group members, which may be difficult when senior management expect them to be loyal to corporate interests instead.

Role conflict can lead to job dissatisfaction, poor group performance, and the rejection of other group members. One recent research study of inter-role conflict found that the more managers and employees disagreed about the employee's role expectations, the more employees experienced work-related stress and felt uncertain about the possibilities of promotion.[7]

Role differentiation

Tony Gunton describes an evolving form of information systems which have the following points in common:

- They involve a number of office workers operating as a team.
- The members of the team need to have shared access to data or to other information which they use to do their jobs.
- They also need to exchange information with the kind of speed and flexibility normally associated with advanced office systems.[8]

The term *work-group systems* is used to describe systems of this type. As these forms of systems develop, the various group members come to play different roles in the social structure – a process called role differentiation. The emergence of different roles in groups is a naturally occurring process. Research[9] confirms that one person emerges in a group who, more than others, helps the group reach its goal. The person plays a 'task-specialist' role. Another group member may emerge who makes each person feel good. Such a person plays a 'socio-emotional' role. The task-specialist and socio-emotional roles played by the group members are composed of several sub-roles – see Figure 4.1.

The whole point of role differentiation is to allow a review of a work group's requirements and the behaviour of its members, not by job title and content, but by a more refined approach to the combinations of task-specialist/socio-emotional roles which constitute successful work groups.

R. Meredith Belbin's research[10] suggests an alternative classification of role types, and makes the important point that the useful people to have in work groups are those who possess strengths and weaknesses which serve a need without duplicating those already there. Work groups are a question of balance. What are needed are not well-balanced individuals, but individuals who balance well with one another.

Task-specialist roles:

Initiator-contributor (recommends new solutions to group problems)
Information seeker (attempts to obtain the necessary facts)
Opinion giver (shares own opinions with others)
Co-ordinator (relates various ideas to the problem at hand)
Energizer (stimulates the group into action when interest drops)

Socio-Emotional Roles:

Harmonizer (mediates group conflicts)
Compromiser (shifts own opinion to create group harmony)
Encourager (praises and encourages others)
Follower (goes along with the ideas of group members)
Expediter (suggests ways the group can operate more smoothly)

Figure 4.1 – Key roles within work groups

Role expectations

The part each person plays in a group is what we mean by the word
'role'. As already stated, a role can be defined as the typical behaviour
which characterizes each person in a specific work group/social context.
An IT manager will make policy decisions about hardware, software,
projects, and specialist personnel – all behaviour expected of the person
occupying the position, or playing the role.

Should a new person assume the same role and have the same
powers as the former incumbent, the same behaviour is expected of this
person. Although specific behaviour of individual IT managers may
vary, certain behaviour (role expectations) are expected of all IT
management role incumbents. That each person in the IT management
appointment recognizes the expectations of the role helps avoid the social
disorganization that would result if clear role expectation did not exist.

Role perception

Job performance in the IT environment will be influenced by each
person's role perceptions. How well each person performs their job will
depend on what is expected of them. A senior analyst/programmer may
believe her task is to train the junior members of her team. But if the
systems and programming manager believes that the same senior
analyst/programmer should be concerned with keeping the project
moving along in line with the agreed schedule, she may be seen as a poor
performer. The seemingly poor performance results from misunderstandings concerning the role the senior analyst/programmer is expected
to play in the organization.

But are we making the process of preparing IT strategies more complex than it need be by introducing the additional requirement for understanding and responding to problems of changing roles, such as ambiguity, conflict, differentiation, expectation, and perception? Received wisdom suggests that simplification makes the unmanageable manageable, that reducing everything to smaller understandable components increases the possibility of success – which is why we recommend viewing the HRM/IT problems via the schema. However, we recognize that over-simplification of the people problems can lead to ignoring some of the more complex issues – the problem is not just shortages of IT skills, there is a need to understand roles. Commenting on the end-user systems environment, Tony Gunton makes the following point:

> As cost/performance of equipment continues to improve, the rate at which organizations can assimilate and gain benefits from IT is no longer determined mainly by whether or not the relevant equipment and software are available. The ability of end-users to master the new technology becomes the key limiting factor. In other words, from the point of view of the managers responsible for organizing the information systems effort, skills in dealing with people are assuming greater weight compared with skills in dealing with technology.[11]

We believe the development of these essential skills for interacting with people demand a greater understanding of the task-specialist and socio-emotional roles played within any work group. Likewise, there are implications for training and development.

Change offers challenges for planners of strategies

When attempting to develop commercial/IT/HRM strategies which involve major changes, the urge to simplify activities continually battles with the urge to gain better control through sophisticated and complex monitoring. In the area of human resource management, simple appraisal procedures compete with complex methods for developing detailed descriptions of jobs, behavioural roles, and psychometric assessments of performance.

Meanwhile, what about all the people caught up in the process of these changes? During our research for this book, we were allowed to view the commercial/IT/HRM strategic plans for several companies. When we asked managers, technical specialists, and end-users about their own formally defined objectives, we found two situations. Some people were buried under dozens of detailed objectives, all part of a corporate responsibility network made up of thousands of links. Others were totally unaware of their objectives in relation to the changes embedded in the strategic plans. In the majority of cases we found everyone was desperate for a simple statement of direction in terms of the implications for their own careers.

Should those who develop commercial/IT/HRM strategies go for 'the big one' or be satisfied with lesser objectives? This is a dilemma which IT managers have lived with for many years – whether information systems should stretch a company's capabilities, or be fully within the capacity of existing personnel. Although small steps can demotivate people, should major strategic changes to commercial/IT/HRM strategies be divided into several small digestible modules?

Our research findings suggest organizations are divided into those who see and develop these strategies as opportunities for building flexibility, more open-mindedness to potential benefits from IT, and a radical proactive approach, whilst others see them as disciplined and effective methods for achieving corporate objectives. Maybe neither view can guarantee success, but some form of 'mapping' is required which allows identification of the objective(s), development of plans for achieving the objective(s), and handling the change problems experienced along the way.

Understanding the nature of technological change in general, and the implications in particular for an organization, should be part of these strategies. How different will the end state be from the present? Will the changes make demands for personal qualities, attitudes, intellectual and vocational abilities not currently present in the organization? Will the changes place more emphasis on certain socio-emotional or task-specialist roles? What are the management dimensions of the potential changes – can the existing management team and its structure handle the implications? What is the organization's metabolic capacity for converting new technology into commercial opportunities? Some parts of a company may be able to handle change more easily than others – how quickly can the organization as a whole move towards the end objective(s)?

For most companies, moving from the current strategy position to that associated with the future, the challenges are going to be mainly in the transition phase. Difficulties associated with supporting current commercial requirements, maintaining an acceptable service level from the IT function, and operating commercially viable HRM policies, will lead to much stress and conflict. It is no good assuming people will act in a sensible and rational manner during the change process. The 'thinkers', who are the people most organizations depend on for successful implementation of new strategies, may well up and off to pastures new in response to attractive opportunities with other companies. Those who remain may be suffering from 'tunnel' vision, or actively supporting the 'resistance movement' which is committed to maintaining the status quo.

The challenge to the commercial/IT/HRM management team is to develop an approach for managing change which not only communicates the organization's objectives in terms of the potential future market and financial benefits, but also helps people to understand and respond in a positive manner to their own personal future within the organization. This latter need will require human resource management policies, which ensure that job redesign, redefining the roles, training, and career development are high on the list of corporate management priorities.

We agree with Andrew Leigh's findings:

- Detecting the needs for organizational change requires a highly developed sensitivity. Too much dependence on earlier visions of the future can be a distraction.
- Generating a will to listen to what may sometimes prove to be unpleasant or hard truths requires much political skill.
- Gaining the support of the sceptics and doubters – all those who support the status quo – calls for great patience.
- Building a critical mass of support from all the isolated commitments to change, suggests the need for an opportunistic approach.
- Transforming the medium and longer-term objectives into specific proposals for current action, must take place as quickly as possible.
- Linking objectives to personal accountability for making it happen is a major priority.
- Relying on many people to sustain the strategic changes is better than relying on just a few.[12]

To overcome the inertia syndrome management must respond to the challenges we have identified.

Change, culture and synergy

Discussions about corporate culture often ignore the fact that within any one company, much less an organization consisting of numerous subsidiary companies, there are several sub-cultures. Our experience, as consultants and practitioners, leads us to believe that many IT functions do not reflect the culture of their parent organizations. We make no judgment about the situation, simply that it appears to be the case. Although many IT functions are closely identified with the commercial objectives of their parents, this does not mean that the ethos of IT or the attitudes of technical specialists have taken on board the culture(s) seen in other parts of the organization.

With the emergence of the end-user systems environment, which allows for much more flexible and adaptable handling of information, we enter into the phase of cultural synergy. But this synergy should not happen just by default. The success or failure of the synergy will be dependent upon how commercial, HRM and IT management respond to the opportunities. Badly managed, the synergy could result in spreading some of the worst cultural aspects of central IT functions. Effectively managed, the synergy will contribute to the future commercial success of an organization.

Managers may find it hard to accept that their own corporate organization will have a number of different sub-cultures and operate in various 'tribal' languages. This is often brought to light when database applications are being developed, and different parts of the organization use different words to describe one specific data field in a computer record. Those involved with implementing data dictionaries will confirm the amount of confusion and conflict which can develop around any attempt to produce a single definition for the data field. Various end-users will have their own descriptions for the field, and IT technical specialists in a central mainframe installation will have generated yet another definition. The message, in all this confusion over a single data field, is that communication in the IT environment, and more so with multiple end-user systems, is as much about language as it is about modems, terminals, local- and wide-area networks.

The commercial/HRM/IT strategies for supporting technological change should not be about establishing conformity of cultures. We must come to terms with the diversity of sub-cultures in our organizations. Being effective and efficient does not demand that everyone in the organization should have identical commercial language or behaviour. Tony Gunton's book *End User Focus*, quoted earlier, illustrates the wide variety of different IT strategies. Each of these has similar cultural elements, but at the same time each possesses unique features. The great contribution from the technological advances is that variety need not be sacrificed to achieve efficiency and effectiveness.

The diversity of cultures and 'tribal' languages is a source of richness – everyone can learn from another person's experiences. We must be watchful, and not allow or confuse the movements to standardize certain aspects of technology to be used as reasons for reducing sub-cultural variety. The way forward is to identify those cultural elements which will be supportive of proactive policies for making effective and efficient change take place. The aspects of 'tribal' language, which lead to implementing appropriate changes, will survive. But, as with the development of languages in general, those elements which fall into disuse will be abandoned by time. Finally, we believe the key concepts for understanding and preparing for change will be communication, level of freedom, and an openness to mutual learning.

Notes and references

1   Tom Peters, *Thriving on Chaos* (Macmillan, 1987).
2   Donald J. Smalter, *Organizing for Change* (Harper and Row, 1972).
3   Andrew Leigh, *Effective Change* (Institute of Personnel Management, 1988).
4   J. E. McGrath, *Stress and Behaviour in Organizations* (Rand McNally, 1976).
5   E. R. Kemery, A. G. Bedeian, K. W. Mossholder and J. Touliatos, 'Outcomes of role stress: a multi-sample constructive replication', *Academy of Management Journal*, 28, pp. 363-375, 1985.
6   R. A. Cooke and D. M. Rousseau, 'Stress and strain from family roles and work-role expectations', *Journal of Applied Psychology*, **69**, pp. 252-260, 1984.
7   V. Berger-Gross and A. I. Kraut, 'Great expectations', *Journal of Applied Psychology*, **69**, pp. 261-271, 1984.
8   Tony Gunton, *Business Information Technology: End User Focus* (Prentice Hall, 1988).
9   K. D. Benne and P. Sheats, 'Functional roles of group members', *Journal of Social Issues*, **4**, pp. 41-49, 1948.
10 R. Meredith Belbin, *Management Teams – Why They Succeed or Fail* (Heinemann, 1981)
11 Tony Gunton, *Business Information Technology: End User Focus* (Prentice Hall, 1988).
12 Andrew Leigh, *Effective Change* (Institute of Personnel Management, 1988).

Further reading

Robert A. Baron, *Behaviour in Organizations – Understanding and Managing the Human Side of Work* (Allyn and Bacon, 1986).
R. M. Kanter, *The Change Masters* (George Allen & Unwin, 1984).
Vincent Nolan, *Open to Change* (MCB Publications, 1981).
C. Pumpkin, *The Essence of Corporate Srategy* (Gower Press, 1987).
William Ouchi, *Theory Z* (Addison-Wesley, 1981).
C. A. Carnall, *The Evaluation of Organizational Change* (Gower Press, 1982).
E. Mumford and D. Henshall, *A Participative Approach to Computer Systems Design* (Associated Business Press, 1979).
E. J. Jones, 'The sensing interview', *Annual Handbook for Group Facilitators*, pp. 213-224 (University Associates, 1973).
G. White, 'Managing stress in organizational change', *WRU Occasional Paper 31*, 1984.
Colin Hastings, Peter Bixby and Randi Chaudhry-Lawton, *Superteams – Blueprint for Organizational Success* (Fontana, 1986).

CHAPTER 5

WHY INVEST IN TRAINING FOR INFORMATION TECHNOLOGY?

Organizations vary in their approach to IT training, be it on-the-job, structured or by accident. Preparing and implementing training programmes which incorporate the needs of the business and the individual is a demanding process.

Training, both technical and managerial, is often unrecognized as a motivator. Commitment to formal training can be a powerful antidote to enticements by other companies. When badly managed, training is expensive and fuels the claims of the *we do not believe in training* lobby.

Too often we hear IT specialists and end-users commenting: 'They would not give me the training to do the job efficiently – just handed me the manual', or 'We were forced to learn from each other and the contract staff'.

End-user training, particularly the use of PC packages, is more easily managed since it is driven by comprehensible and perceived needs, and could form part of the common training programmes for whole commercial/industrial sectors. This places the ball firmly in the court of the various business associations.

Training/learning modules could become an essential feature of the applications developed for the emerging end-user systems environment. But those producing these modules will need to understand the learning process, and be experienced in the use of 'course-authoring' software.

Computer-based-training, audio-visual programmes, expert systems, and interactive laser disc facilities, can provide new levels of flexibility in scheduling training. But the new training technology could dazzle management, to the point of forgetting the true objectives of training.

The effect of governmental initiatives for technology training within education have yet to be quantified, but they spotlight a need not recognized fully by business.

Background

Training can be defined as 'the systematic development of the attitude/knowledge/skill pattern required by an individual in order to perform adequately a given task or job'. But some managers say it is not worth training people because staff move on all too quickly, maybe even to competitors. However, if management do not train staff they may lose them anyway! Do something you lose, do nothing you lose. Are the only winners the training establishments, the staff agencies and the candidates who land the next lucrative job?

Every report about skills shortages suggests that the answer is more training. We believe the answer does not lie simply in training because skill shortages are a symptom of a much deeper problem contained in the management of the human resources.

Training is necessary but potentially futile if managers do not develop and maintain the critical mass of knowledge and experience in their companies. Sending people on courses alone is at best ineffective, and in reality only placates the conscience of management to respond to the governmental admonishments regarding the lack of investment in training.

Cost is one of management's arguments against training. It is considered to be an investment with a dubious return. We agree that throwing money at the problem, without an appropriate strategy for retaining the body of expertise, is to spit in the wind!

Those with expertise should be constantly developing those lacking skills. Experienced staff should be required to do so as part of their job. Ownership of knowledge must not be allowed to become the prerogative of the few – you should not keep your knowledge to yourself. Part of the value of people to a company is the willingness to share knowledge. This must not be seen as diminishing their prospects or security, but as increasing their value to the company. We would suggest that IT provides an ideal environment in which to launch this concept, since the natural fears/caution regarding survival are less acute because of the continual demand for skills and knowledge on the open labour market.

Despite the reactionary attitudes of some managers to training, we believe that there is a growing awareness of the need for training and retraining as many national economies experience the change from industrial to post-industrial society. Structural changes in economies during the past twenty years, from manufacturing to service industries, and the rapid growth and sophistication of technology present a major challenge at national as well as organizational level. Career patterns are changing. It is unlikely that anyone starting work now will have the same career for life. A once and for all initial training will no longer be appropriate. Rather people will need to be trained to adapt. Training and retraining will be necessary throughout a person's working life.

There is no doubt that government policy gives impetus to the development of a more systematic approach to training within companies and the more formal organization of the training function. In the UK the 1964 Industrial Training Act was brought in because of the shortage of skilled people and the ineffectiveness of the existing training effort. By the time all but six of the twenty-three Industrial Training Boards set up by that Act had been abolished in 1981 their levy/grant system had encouraged companies to undertake training programmes. Their advice on training and their Group Training Schemes had assisted small companies. Their research and publications had helped to improve the standard of training in many organizations.

Although relevant and effective training is only one of the variables influencing business activities, the benefits of training can be expected in many areas. Benefits for the ever expanding IT environment will accrue in:

* Helping new employees to learn their jobs more quickly and effectively – improving work performance of existing employees – increasing the volume of work achieved – reducing work errors – reducing labour turnover – increasing job satisfaction – replacing obsolescent skills with new abilities – reducing accidents – increasing the flexibility of the work force – providing career development opportunities – improving the corporate image.
* Assisting the implementation of change.

These benefits are even more significant, rather than less so, if an organization is affected by recession or tight budgetary constraints, and training can still be justified as a good business investment.

Transfer of knowledge as a strategy

An American specialist software company operates worldwide through franchises. These franchises sell, install and support customers using modules of the product, which is a multi-function applications system.

In Western Europe, due in part to the narrow specialism of the application, franchises have difficulty in maintaining teams for installation and support. The franchises confine their activity to selling and technical reference for installers. However, a franchise never provides first-level support, but offers clients the use of their recommended installers – nominated software houses who will install and support according to an agreed level of service.

In these software houses, it is imperative to maintain a stable skills resource covering all modules of the application. Failure to provide an agreed level of service would result in litigation.

As skills and experience of the products are developed, staff are subjected to high levels of inducement from clients and other software houses, to leave and bring their knowledge with them.

Training courses are readily available from the franchiser, but they are expensive in time and cost. This discourages most users of the package, and influences them to lean on outside suppliers for support.

The software house in our example acquires its skill base by maintenance of a nucleus of expertise from which knowledge is shared and support provided. For each critical module or function of the application, a minimum of three skilled staff can be identified: one 'expert' and two others at varying levels of development.

Every member of the team will have exposure to a minimum of three modules. Development is based on continual change in responsibility, be it seniority level or module. For staff other than the 'expert', it is normal to experience two changes per year, either to broaden knowledge by learning a further module or by moving up the support structure of a particular module. All team members are imbued with the importance of mutual support and development moves are handled in a similar way.

Such an environment is supportive to new entrants. Trainees with end-user or commercial experience are brought in, allocated to an experienced person – not necessarily one of the 'experts' – who tutors and supports them through initial training courses and provides consolidation experience via current projects.

The source of skill at graduate or trainee level is modest in initial cost. Training is costly, and salaries are progressed by six-monthly reviews for thirty-six months, to maintain market value. The costs of this approach must be considered against the business issue of revenue from maintenance contracts. There are no anomalies with the salaries of comparable staff, hence the ease of movement at the senior level.

Whilst movement away from the application occurs at a senior level, and 'poaching' is most successful at the 'expert' level, there is sufficient space for trainees to reach up: it is unusual for junior team members to leave, despite the sizeable inducements from customers or other software houses. The track record of their predecessors demonstrates the career development value of the knowledge transfer process, and they are cynical of the long-term benefits of too early a move to client organizations frantic to exploit their knowledge, but not committed to their career development. If the loss rate to the external market accelerated, no doubt this approach would be reviewed, but it has survived six years of pressure on this much sought-after knowledge and experience.

Bringing together the training requirements of the organization and the individual

Rather than writing about training from the theoretical point of view, we will explore the subject through a practical example which contains all the elements required for establishing successful training strategies.

Setting the scene

A large international organization, which manufactures high technology products, reached its present successful position by a series of mergers over the years. It employs some 23,000 people in the UK (over a number of different sites) and overseas. It has some 15,000 customers. Group functions look after the company as a whole and the various divisions are split by function or product.

Historically, the organization has been associated with a specific area of high technology, a market which has now stabilized. Development effort has shifted to more rapidly growing sectors of the technology's market.

One division is a major key to the company's future success. It employs some 1,200 people in total, mostly split into small sub-units of 120 people, each developing a particular product. The sub-units are divided into segments containing approximately fifty people, which are further divided into sectors consisting of up to twenty-five people. Within each sub-unit all the necessary management functions – i.e. development and marketing – are grouped together under one manager. The sub-units, being based on a project team approach, allow rapid reaction to technological change with minimum upheaval to the division and the parent company. Changes can be incorporated into products needed by customers and marketed in a targeted commercial/industrial areas. The sub-units are task orientated and re-form on completion of a project. A sub-unit is responsible for seeing the project through and has a profit line to pursue.

Most of the division's 1,200 employees are engaged on developmental work, apart from staff involved in running the building, or supporting the personnel and training function.

Sub-unit employees are graduates, largely engineers and programmers who develop hardware and software to support the various high technology products. The organizational climate is decentralized, delegative and informal.

As to the corporate culture, the parent company has its bureaucratic aspects in the Head Office functions, to maintain certain common standards throughout the organization, but the division has considerable autonomy in its operation within the framework of corporate policy. It has complete autonomy in administering its budget and manpower allocation. Insofar as its organization revolves round particular projects in the sub-units, it is a task culture.[1] The sub-units are not part of a matrix structure[2] but self-contained operations with a high degree of decentralization.

It is not surprising that training is regarded as a priority for the division, to keep abreast of the latest technology, to build up team morale, and to convert technology into what the market requires.

Analysing the training needs of the organization

A need implies that something is lacking, that there is a shortfall between what is happening and what should be happening. A training need implies that this gap can be bridged by training. Training must be the correct tool for the need. It is first necessary to ensure that shortfalls will be met by training rather than by other means, such as work reorganization or better employee selection and placement. It may be that a need will be met by a combination of approaches, including training.

It is possible to analyse training needs from different viewpoints within the organization. Organizational training needs can be analysed by looking at the corporate business plans, the divisional business plans and plans for individual employees. Occupational training needs can be analysed by looking at agreed schemes of training linked to career paths. In addition to 'planned' training, ad hoc training needs are generated by particular situations that arise unexpectedly.

How are training needs analysed at the organizational level within the parent company? The company does not take the total approach of examining its entire operation from scratch, nor does it take as its starting point apparently pressing problem areas. Rather, training needs are derived from company and divisional business plans and strategies.

The business plan for the company indicates the projected areas of training needs for the next year to five years. In a rapidly changing high technology environment there is a major degree of uncertainty and it will be appreciated that business plans may have to change rapidly. Accurate predictions of emergent knowledge and skills for more than one year ahead are therefore difficult to make, though trends may be established for a longer period.

Business plans for the company can indicate actions in such areas as:

- SALES TARGETS: market to be attacked, areas e.g. UK, Europe, world-wide; size of company to be approached; particular types of company to be approached, e.g local government, retailing; specialized market sectors; market share.
- PRODUCT MIXES: what will be the output balance between the various technological products?
- MANUFACTURING POLICY: which components are to be made in and which bought out; which software to be written in-house and which bought out; what will be the effect of new technology on manufacturing processes?

Training needs will be established for the company on the basis of these plans – proactive in the sense that they will be based on what the company wants to achieve. The business plans indicate areas where training needs will increase and also areas where they will be cut back.

The business plan for the division evolves around the various sub-units' projects, and these determine most of the training needs for the division – the training function has to react to these needs.

Each division produces a written training and development strategy based on the divisional business plan and the divisional manpower plan for the next two years. From these plans it derives key training and development implications. Each strategy looks at the role of the division in the company business plan, and from that together with assumptions about its future role it looks at general and specific implications for training. A typical list of specific needs is given in Figure 5.1.

These requirements would then have to be translated into specific courses, on- or off-site, for particular individuals.

Technical training requirements

> Microprocessor applications
> VLSI technology
> Cost-effective design methods
> Systems software (operating systems)
> Programming skills
> Keeping abreast of world-wide technical development
> Operating advanced test/evaluation systems

Management training requirements

> Project planning, costing and control
> Corporate financial systems
> Presentation and communication techniques
> Inter-personal and group skills.

Figure 5.1 Typical list of training needs

Analysing the training needs of the individual

When it comes to individual training plans, the divisional business plan requirements would be matched up with individual needs. Individual needs would be decided during staff appraisals which indicate the strengths and weaknesses of performance over the previous period and compare that performance against agreed objectives. Consideration is also given to career aims and expectations. It is normal practice for this process to take place several times a year, with training and development plans for the individual being updated during the year when the process is completed.

Succession planning based upon an organization review mechanism is carried out for senior levels of management, and development plans are produced for those managers with succession potential.

In some particular job bands, agreed schemes of training are linked to these career paths, e.g. salesman, technical authors, management. Much of the training for individuals following these career paths is planned on this basis. These schemes have been developed in the company, and may be amended as training needs in these areas change, but they are associated with a particular job and progression in that job. It is incumbent on each job holder to go through the recognized programme of training for that job, but the pace and perhaps sequence of courses can be varied between individuals. All managers for example have to progress through a management development programme as appropriate, ranging from an induction course for new managers to a Stage 4 course for very senior management. When managers become eligible for the next period of training, the training manager contacts them with possible dates.

Ad hoc training needs

Ad hoc training needs may arise from a policy decision at corporate level or in reaction to a particular local situation.

When the company decided to adopt a new commercial operating system rather than write their own operating system, there was a widespread demand from managers urging the Training Manager to organize specific training for their staff.

A 'need' can emerge as people go about their jobs, some problem or fault occurs that highlights a shortfall between actual performance and required performance. If on analysis a training need is indicated, then some training would be devised and actioned. For example, the company twice conducted an employee opinion survey, and for both years employees were critical of the communications systems within the division. The Divisional Director responded by asking the Training Manager to organize team briefing training sessions for all the appropriate levels of management. Similarly, on two occasions individual grievances reached divisional director level. This led to an examination of how lower levels of management were dealing with grievance handling and more generally with performance appraisals and a whole range of other inter-personal skills. A course was devised more far-reaching in scope and also with a more positive approach than that indicated by the original issue. Again, the technical authoring function found that they spent time and effort training technical authors who promptly left the company for more attractive short-term benefits. This led to arranging more career development training programmes so that technical authors could see a clear career progression within the company, which helped to solve the problem.

An ad hoc training need could arise on a more individual basis. An employee could be reprimanded for poor performance, but every effort is made by the company to try to improve the individual's performance by an agreed programme of training.

An employee might himself recognize the need for some training and initiate a request for it, either internally within the company or from an outside source. If the external training would help him in his job skills or develop his potential, the company will provide time off and possibly financial assistance, for example to study part time for professional qualifications.

Policies for training

Company training policy

In the booklet given to every employee, the company explains its basic approach to business and commits itself to 'people' development. It does not regard itself as just in the high technology sector, selling sophisticated equipment, but in the 'knowledge industry' – marketing a total solution. In this context, the skill and abilities of people must be constantly developed to keep the company in the forefront of new technology.

Management responsibility for training

When the business plans have been decided and the budgets allocated for the division, it is the line managers who are responsible for ensuring that their own staff receive adequate training and career development. Authority for training and development is delegated throughout the division with each level of management responsible for improving the knowledge, skills and performance of staff who report directly to them. Each manager is accountable for the identification and implementation of the training and development needs/requirements and can call upon the specialist training and development resource within the division or company.

Training facilities

Various facilities exist for training within the company and the division.

At corporate level, there are two in-company training centres. One has its own computing facilities and is concerned with high technology product training. It also offers courses on various management skills – effective communication, appraisals, etc., whilst the second site is concerned with training sales personnel. The Division has a 'learning centre' with a library and self-teach facilities based on audio-visual aids. Most of the self-teach packages are produced by external suppliers, although the company is developing a capability for computer-based authoring of courses.

The training budget

Financial resources are allocated to the division for training on the basis of the division's business plans, manpower plans, and the training and development strategy it adopts as a result.

The divisional training budget runs into several hundred thousand pounds. It has to be justified on the basis of the business plans of each sub-unit in the division. The training budgets are not always cut back in the budgetary round. Recently, the Managing Director told the division it was not spending enough on training! The Training Manager administers the training budget for the division and charges out course costs to the appropriate sub-unit.

Organization of the training function

There is one training unit – Group Training – which reports at corporate level, with a manager and approximately six staff. They are responsible for developing and running a core development programme for management training within the company.

The division has its own training function headed by a manager and his assistant. Prior to the implementation of the sub-unit organizational approach, the training function had a staff of sixteen for 3,500 people (ratio 1 : 218), now there are two staff for 1,200 people (ratio 1 : 600).

Role of the training function

The size of the training function in relation to the people covered means that the Training Manager is not able to develop as proactive a role as he would like in divisional training. With a staff of two, resources are limited. The Training Manager cannot become too deeply involved in helping managers to analyse in detail departmental training needs, or in following up how well learning has been transferred to the actual work situation.

The Training Manager sees his primary role as managing the organization of training for the division. He is available to give specialist advice, if required, on training to divisional management, other line managers and individual employees. The Training Manager's other function is career counselling. He knows what training courses are available, the best courses for particular needs, which are worthwhile, which are best value for money. He has built up this experience and expertise over the years. All formal training undertaken in the division goes through the Training Manager, although a sub-unit might organize an informal course for itself. Some of the sub-units have a training liaison person, part time, looking after training.

Responsibility for deciding where a course is to be run and who is to run it lies with the Training Manager. It could be on-site; it could use corporate facilities; it could be external. The trainers may be the company's own personnel, specialists from the suppliers of hardware and software, or external training consultants.

For on-site courses, the Training Manager is responsible for finding people to run the course, setting up the course, and advertising it throughout the Division to make up the numbers.

Standard company induction courses are run at one of the corporate training centres for the new graduate entry each year. Some technical training in support of the various microprocessors used in the Division's products is bought out. The universities are used to provide 'state of the art' topics. Training in marketing is supported by in-house trainers, but additional instructors are brought in from the USA.

Training records

The training function is supported by an end-user system which allows all divisional training records to be held in a database. The training record for each person includes identification of the individual, details of all courses attended (title, length, costs, dates), and a charge code. These records can be accessed according to any selection criteria, such as type of training or charge code, or an individual's training record can be examined on demand.

Training policies in operation

Responsibility for training

The line managers are responsible for ensuring that their staff receive appropriate training, but many of them take a short-term view. They want to utilize their new graduate intake straight away. Apart from the compulsory induction training they are sometimes reluctant to spare them on courses, and are liable to cancel courses at short notice on account of a 'higher priority' business need. The managers are under such pressure for projects to be completed that formal training is often put off, being replaced by on-the-job lunchtime talks, use of videos in the learning centre, etc. The Training Manager would like to see managers not only accountable in theory for training but actually held accountable for it at their own performance appraisals. They are accountable if their product is late or receive commendation if it is on time or ahead of schedule, but this is not the case regarding the training they should have instigated.

Who is to be trained?

It is company policy that every employee should receive sufficient training to enable him to do his job properly and to develop his career. Inevitably priorities have to be decided. It is not financially possible to guarantee every employee, say, two weeks training per year; this would cost the division some £2.5 million. If, however, it was vital to the company that one person receive particular training, he would get it, even if it amounted to seven or eight weeks in the year. Where funds are limited, priority naturally has to go to areas of most importance to the business.

Work group training initiatives

The division has some trade union participation in the formulation of training policies. Earlier in the 1980s, the divisional management set up a 'Career Development Working Party' because of union pressure. Both parties agreed that there was a lack of forward planning for training and career development as technology and the company's business strategy changed, and that this gave serious cause for concern. The Working Party has fifty per cent trade union membership, with a sector manager as chairman and the Training Manager, together with other representatives from the personnel function. The view of the manager and people in a sub-unit are investigated. The objectives are:

- To review career development and training procedures, suggest how

they can be made effective and who will make the changes.
* To make recommendations and to propose implementation plans.
* To identify differences between the skills that development staff need now and additional skills they will need in the future.
* To identify current skill needs and propose training programmes.

The Working Party reported back and action plans were approved but could not be implemented immediately because of certain financial constraints. However, the proposals, particularly proposals encouraging self development, were incorporated into the divisional training strategy.

Quality circles have been introduced into the division. They do not usually address themselves to formal training but courses are arranged for quality circle leaders who decide they would like some training.

Type of training

As to be expected in a high technology company, the emphasis is placed on technical training. However, recently there has been an interesting change in the proportions of technical to development training in the division. Technical training used to be first priority and amounted to two-thirds of total training. As a result of a corporate decision that middle management should perform more efficiently, the proportion of management and personal skills training has been increased to almost half the total.

Re-training

Skill obsolescence in the light of technological advances is not a major problem in the division. Being mainly research and development, they are in an area of technology that is changing rapidly all the time and they are part of it. The main skill requirement of engineeers and programmers is an ability to adapt and learn quickly. For electronic engineers their area of knowledge is computer design where the main changes are miniaturization and cheaper production. Programmers already have a good range of programming languages when they join the division. They can learn new programming languages quickly and they adapt to the more gradual systems software changes over the years. In both areas the actual knowledge required changes but the skills required remain the same.

In contrast, however, are computer service engineers who have experienced dramatic changes in their job skills, involving them in a very extensive reprofiling exercise. This need was thrown up by a company skills audit. A corporate team was sent into the division, they designed courses, carried them out and also trained the service engineering function to run the courses themselves. Each individual engineer was assessed in terms of abilities and suitability for available vacancies – some were successfully reprofiled, but older engineers with the biggest skills gap left the organization.

Sponsorship of further education

The company encourages individuals to undertake relevant courses of further education. It will sponsor and pay the fees for Open University courses, evening classes and part-time courses. A number of employees have been sponsored for a one-year M.Sc. course.

It is divisional policy to sponsor several students at any one time on their first degree course. A grant is paid for each academic term and the Training Manager arranges for the students to be employed in the division to gain work experience. Some of the students take up a job in the division on completion of their course if this is mutually agreeable.

Training programmes

How are training needs and policies converted into training programmes in the context of the company? All the main training programmes in which divisional employees participate will be mentioned briefly. Two will be discussed in more detail, namely the Management Development Programme and the Technical Author's Training Programme. The latter provides a good example of a systematic training programme – both technical and developmental – for all its employees, and one which has succeeded in achieving its objectives. These programmes are associated with particular job skills and career paths. In addition, we shall look at ad hoc type courses that have resulted from particular problems arising.

Graduate induction

Graduates already have technical skills in computer design or programming when they join the company. The first prerequisite is therefore the one-week compulsory induction course, run in October and November, the traditional time for new graduate intake. The division is allocated a number of places on this course. If places are allocated for November, graduates could have already spent some time working in the division.

The objective with the graduate entry to the division is to enable them to make a significant contribution to a project as quickly as possible. The induction training is a formal course to introduce them to the company, its products and markets. It is sales orientated as the largest proportion of graduates are from the Sales Division. It involves investigating a mythical customer's needs and putting up a sales proposal.

Soon after joining, many graduates attend a one-week graduate skills workshop involving training in personal skills, organization of work, presentation, and report writing. Graduates could subsequently be sent on a one-week course on new product orientation, as and when necessary.

Clerical and secretarial staff

Clerical and secretarial staff are given some local information when they commence their jobs, but receive no formal induction to the work environment. If appropriate, they are given two two-day courses on word processing and receive instruction about the use of the electronic mail terminals.

Sales and marketing

Marketing graduates in the division undergo a rigid two-year training programme at the corporate training establishments. Their managers are committed to sending staff on these courses and cannot allow them to opt out, as they tend to do in some of the divisional sub-units involving other graduate staff. Four or five faculty members from a university in the USA run these courses. With a highly volatile, not to say turbulent, market environment for the high technology products, marketing is crucial to the company's survival – what does the market want? how much? at what price? etc.

Personnel and finance

There is no formal training programme for personnel or finance staff. Some people may be studying for professional qualifications, but the remainder do not participate in courses specially designed for their requirements.

Management development programme

The main objectives of the Management Development Programme are:

- to ensure that all managers are aware of the company's management approach required of them and the standard philosophy of the company.
- to develop where necessary general management and inter-personal skills as well as technical skills.

The corporate training function, in conjunction with a major business school, devised a series of training modules which all managers are required to attend at an appropriate stage of their management career.

With the introduction of a formalized statement of corporate philosophy, it was necessary to restructure and reorganize the courses into four stages. At each stage there is a core programme plus additional modules, some of which are optional and some of which are obligatory.

The Management Development Programme is based on the company's ten obligations of a manager, shown in Figure 5.2.

1. To be effective business operations managers and effective people managers. It is only in this way that results can be optimized as well as targets achieved.
2. To possess detailed knowledge of the company's objectives and strategies. They must be able to relate them to the high technology business sector, to competitors, to customers and to products. They must communicate these objectives to members of their own sub-units to enable them to see their roles, responsibilities and standards required.
3. To be able to meet the challenge of predicting, managing and exploiting change with foresight, judgment and leadership.
4. To ensure that their own work tasks and those of their staff generate high value outputs that create a demonstrable impact on business results.
5. To stimulate team work by developing individual talents, building on team ideas and know-how and gain commitment by the way of listening (hearing), involving and communicating.
6. To ensure that optimum use is made of current skills and develop career progression plans.
7. To think in terms of opportunities rather than problems, be willing to attack tasks in a positive way and encourage his staff to do the same.
8. To set the framework for creativity: freedom to challenge the traditional and try out new ideas in a supportive environment.
9. To recognize difficult issues and face up to them quickly. By openly and constructively discussing problems as soon as they arise a manager can reduce the risk of long-term negative attitudes.
10. To appraise their own management actions and the way they as individuals, and their work units, contribute to business results.

Figure 5.2 Ten obligations of a manager

The whole Management Development Programme consists of just over twenty different courses and workshops, the majority of which must be attended. There are a number of optional modules which are directly linked to each manager's specialist area.

The course is structured so that it can act as a forum on corporate strategies in world markets. It deals with real problems facing the company, not theoretical situations.

Technical authors

The Technical Publications Unit publishes its own staff training guide which gives anyone joining the sub-unit a complete picture of the training they can expect to receive during their career. The objective is to provide not only necessary technical training but also career development and management training. Retention of technical authors was a problem when individuals could not foresee how their careers would develop within the function, and they tended to leave for short-term advantages elsewhere.

A full training programme is in operation, but it responds to each individual's needs. Training requirements are discussed with technical authors at least twice a year, and the appraisal is not signed off by the reviewing manager unless it contains a statement of training requirements and an individual training plan has been lodged with the Training Manager.

Author training is geared to giving specific skills in technical authoring – programming, printing technology, keyboard skills, word processing, and desktop publishing. Most of their technical training takes place at one of the corporate training centres, but some specialized external courses and seminars are used. In addition there are courses about the company's products, with specific reference to those produced by the division.

Ad hoc training programmes

The needs for additional types of training have been quite wide. Communications problems within the Division led to the Training Manager organizing some team briefing sessions in conjunction with the Industrial Society.

Two grievances reached director level as a result of managers' inability to deal with the performance problems of their staff. A course was developed with an external training consultant on the subject of 'Improving staff performance', and included:

- Setting objectives and analysing achievements.
- Improving performance.
- Selection interviewing.

Although most training courses are an integrated part of the company's formal training programme, there is no objection to courses filling surprise needs.

Evaluation of training programmes

What measures can be taken to evaluate training programmes? To what extent does evaluation of training programmes take place in the division?

Evaluation of training programmes can be viewed from several different perspectives – validation/feedback/reinforcement, budgeting, cost-effective training, cost/benefit analysis, and best mix of cost/benefits.

Validation, feedback and reinforcement

At the lowest level a check has to be made, at some point after the training has taken place, to see whether the training objectives have been achieved. The more measurable the objectives, the easier it is to check whether the required learning has taken place.

Many courses either have built-in validation or a definite follow-up check. This is often the case with courses based on information technology itself. In the case of the Management Development Programme we mentioned earlier, pre-course questionnaires are filled in by the manager being trained, one of his staff, a peer manager and his immediate superior. The training is evaluated when similar questionnaires are completed six months later and the two sets compared.

Feedback is also sought after the team briefing sessions. When a particular message should have been communicated by team briefing, the divisional personnel manager checks with the Trade Union representatives, *Were you told?*, to determine how many employees actually received the message down the line.

The in-house technical authors' course allows for immediate feedback. As a trainee completes an exercise, his or her answer is compared with a sample answer. This provides a starting point for the discussion of the exercise. There is no single 'right answer' and it is the discussion itself that is regarded as one of the most important elements of the training.

On other courses, participants return with an action plan for their own sub-unit, which they are required to implement.

After a course on 'Improving staff performance', managers go off and implement objectives. Subsequently, samples of outputs produced by them, e.g. performance appraisals, improvement plans, are reviewed with the Training Manager.

Budgeting

This involves the recording and controlling of training costs, which is necessary if a higher level of cost/benefit analysis is to be undertaken.

The divisional training budget is agreed with Corporate Planning after a number of possible 'budgetary rounds'. Each sub-unit manager has to put up a business case for his share of the training budget, which has to be approved. He has to indicate how much is to be spent on what, and what returns he envisages for it. The sub-unit training budget is part of its costs and could increase in one year, if new methodologies and products are introduced, or could be cut in another. Training expenditure has varied from as little as £1,800 to as much as £21,000 between sub-units in a half-year period. The Training Manager keeps a record of the costs of all formal courses and charges courses out to the appropriate unit/cost centres. He ensures that the units keep within their training budgets.

Cost-effective training

The Training Manager also compares different courses and training methods and makes choices on the basis of cost-effectiveness. This applies particularly to the costing of on-site and external courses. If only one person required a particular course, it would be cheaper to send them on an external course; if there were demand from ten people it would be cheaper to set up an on-site course. For example, an external course might cost £350 per head, whilst a similar course run on site for the ten people could cost £870 in total. To fill an on-site course and make it cost effective to run, the Training Manager advertises the course throughout the Division.

Cost/benefit analysis

It is an unfortunate fact that training costs are always more readily assessable in financial terms than training benefits. Establishment costs the cost of running the training function within the company (salaries, accommodation); marginal costs – the costs of carrying out one training activity (fees, expenses); interference costs – the losses to output incurred by a sub-unit as a result of sending someone on a course – can all be calculated.

Tangible benefits, arising from increasing a person's technical competence, e.g. typing speeds, can be measured and given a direct monetary value. In this instance the benefits of training can be measured in terms of the job performance of the individual. However, moving further away from training inputs makes it more difficult to measure the effects of training, as these effects become modified by an increasing number of external influences. The individual's increased typing speed may have no benefit at all at departmental or company level, if external factors prevent the individual's extra skills from being utilized more

Best mix of cost/benefits

This would require information on costs of training, benefits calculated in money terms and the cost of alternative training methods. It attempts to take an overall look at training investment where there are a number of training objectives to achieve (e.g. management and technical). The company looked at this aspect in the sense that it decided to allocate more resources to management training in relation to technical training. This is part of corporate policy; the company clearly expects benefits to emerge from more investment in management training. The Training Manager would always be reviewing the costs of alternative training methods as part of his cost-effectiveness decisions.

As yet traditional courses have not been displaced by alternative training methods such as 'open learning' techniques. The company has not itself developed any self-teach software packages, but major use is made of audio-visual facilities during informal training sessions.

Comments on one company's experience of extensive training programmes

All training functions would prefer to feel they are working in a proactive mode. However, the harsh realities of the business environment do not always allow this to be so. The Training Manager in the Division finds himself with a reactive role because:

- The training function consists of two people only and he has insufficient resources to take a more proactive line.
- Corporate training decisions have to be carried out.
- Divisional demands resulting from business plans and projects have to be met.
- Much of the training is already pre-determined by being associated with particular job streams.
- Ad hoc situations arise which call for a response in terms of devising appropriate training.

Given a free hand and more resources the Training Manager would like to see:

- The level of training increased throughout the Division.
- A more formal graduate training programme in which graduates move about more in the division, say, every two years to broaden their experience; also a move out of the division for three months' secondment to Customer Support to see the environment in which their high technology products work. Some graduates have been in the Division for ten to fifteen years and have never met a customer!
- All graduate recruitment by means of sponsored students at university. In 1984, sixty-five graduates were taken on, and in 1985 the number was forty-five – only three or four of whom were sponsored students.
- A broader programme of training for managers to give them wider

experience; they tend to be narrowly technical and no high-flying managers have come from the development sub-units.

If the level of training were increased in the division it might be possible to include more formal training for the areas of secretarial, finance and personnel.

Conclusions about making investments in training

We believe that training alone will not solve the human resource problems experienced in the information technology environment. The solution is associated with maintaining the critical mass of knowledge in each organization. Training will be an essential component in the building of effective corporate strategies (commercial, human resource management, and information technology), but throwing money, time and effort at badly defined objectives will only lead to more trouble.

Notes and references

1   A task culture seeks to bring together the appropriate skills at the right level, and allow the human resources a high degree of control over their work.
2   In a matrix structure, a project team is permanently cemented into either a two or three-dimensional system of corporate controls (technical stream, job types, and project activities).

Further reading

D. Torrington and L. Hall, *Personnel Management – A New Approach* (Prentice Hall, 1987).
John Kenney, Eugene Donnelly and Margaret Reid, *Manpower Training and Development* (Institute of Personnel Management, 1983).

CHAPTER 6

MOTIVATION – IS IT MORE THAN STICKS AND CARROTS?

The motivation of IT personnel is frequently challenged and their loyalty to employers questioned. Why do they choose a career in IT? What are the qualities of the successful? What is their motivation? Over the years graduates have displayed a variety of reasons for entering IT. Initially it was the opportunity to display numeracy, the security of an expanding field, and more recently a growing tendency to see IT as a possible route into executive management – an alternative to accountancy. Now there is an emerging wish to interact with business people and solve their business problems through technology.

Maslow's theory of motivation postulates a hierarchy of needs, from physiological needs, through security, social, and ego to self-fulfilment needs. This suggests that we should examine the potential of IT roles and careers to satisfy the needs of current and future employees. Herzberg's motivational model (recognition, achievement and responsibility) confirms that pay alone will provide only short-term satisfaction.

Consider a typical recruitment to resignation cycle. A programmer is recruited against the need for a particular technical skill – a specific language, hardware, or operating environment, and maybe particular applications experience. Selection criteria will invariably be biased towards the technical needs. There is little opportunity to consider personal motivation beyond a basic expression of future aspirations. The programmer has been recruited for the skill which will now be exploited. A higher salary will have enticed this person and an expectation will have been created when career development was mentioned during the interviews. But the satisfaction element of the increased earnings soon fades, the build-up of work pressure due to staff shortages, amended specifications and lead times, together with changing priorities, negates any chance of personal satisfaction from achievement. Inevitably, the advertisements in the computing journals, offering the prospect of an escape from the morass, produces the resignation. A costly scenario for company and individual.

The need to change, to take on new concepts, abandon technologies acclaimed only months before, is part of most IT careers. The changes are often fundamental yet not always recognized as such. IT people are expected to be flexible and adaptable. But there is a failure to recognize that whilst there is great capacity to adapt within individuals' motivational pattern or life script, they may be operating in their current role at the extremes of such a pattern. Further pressure to bend in a particular direction may take them far from their own natural pattern with disastrous consequences.

Background

If two people are doing a similar job in a similar environment why does one do it better than another, perhaps much better? Differences of performance in similar jobs could reflect differences of ability, skill and experience or reflect differences in motivation.

But what is motivation? One definition suggests that it is a set of processes which energize a person's behaviour and direct him or her towards attaining some goal, or put more simply 'getting people to do willingly and well those things which have to be done'.

The complexity of individual motives and attitudes makes any generalization difficult, nevertheless a number of social scientists have put forward theories of motivation. Management has taken an increasing interest in these theories in an attempt to explain employee motivation at work. If these theories can be seen to have validity they will be of more than passing academic interest to management, faced with deciding on the most effective incentives and rewards for directing employees towards achievement of organizational goals. When we approach the topic of motivation, it is important to appreciate that there are two different areas for our attention. First, there is the need to understand the process of motivation – the various theories which have been developed. Second, because these theories have to be applied to the practical problems faced in our organizations, including the ever expanding IT environment, we have to understand the different techniques which facilitate their implementation.

An IT environment, be it a central data processing function, a distributed information system, an office utility network, or an end-user computing environment, consists of people who are faced with the basic needs to avoid hunger, seek relationships with others thus avoiding loneliness, and to be able to please others by their behaviour. These people are faced with choices: a hungry person chooses between a sandwich in the company's snackbar, or a more expensive meal in the company's restaurant; a lonely person will seek the company of one friend or another; to please an end-user, a programmer may work especially hard on an essential computer project. Each of us makes intentional choices and selects specific objectives, in addition to which we have to face the demands of reaching the goals.

Motivation is a very difficult concept to observe directly because it is a hypothetical construct. Our motives can only be inferred on the basis of behaviour. But motivation and job performance are not synonymous. Performance is influenced by many factors – skill, ability and working conditions – not just motivation[1]. It would be a mistake to assume that an IT function's record for missing project delivery dates is the result of poor motivation. Motivation is a determinant in the performance of work, but it is not the only determinant.

To look at motivation is to look at a kaleidoscope of endless combinations, some of which may be in conflict. A programmer who is motivated to please an end-user may not do so fully because of the need to retain a favourable relationship with fellow IT specialist personnel. A behaviour which satisfies one motive may conflict with the satisfaction of another motive. This can be the case for an IT worker whose behaviour on a specific task conflicts with the things he or she may be motivated to do for his or her career.[2]

We stress these points about the complexity of motivation because they must be incorporated into any theory of work motivation which is to have any practical value for the IT environment.

Is it possible to motivate people working in the IT environment?

In the introduction to this chapter we referred to how the attitudes of IT personnel are frequently challenged and their loyalty to employers questioned. Claims such as these raise questions about the extent to which some IT workers, at least, care about work and are motivated to perform it. Whether IT workers are motivated or not by the work they do has important implications for management developing corporate strategies. Can we motivate others directly, or is it a case of limiting those of our actions which lead to the demotivation of others? There are two opposing views about work and human nature. These have been analysed in depth by Douglas McGregor.³ The traditional management view is known as *Theory X* which is a cynical and pessimistic under-standing of human motivation at work. In essence it suggests that workers are lazy, selfish, lacking in ambition, not interested in the re-quirements of the organization – unmotivated to work. McGregor argues that X-style managers treat workers in a very harsh coercive manner. Ultimately, this results in workers behaving in the very way managers had hoped to minimize in the first place.

The alternative view, known as *Theory Y*, is a more positive, enlight-ened and optimistic view of human nature. The theory proposes that workers want responsibilities and are not passive, they wish to develop their skills and use their abilities in accordance with the needs of the organization. Much of this will depend on the type of policies and motivational systems practised by management, both of which should be geared to assisting workers to develop their own potential. Given these two requirements, IT workers (managers, technical specialists, and end-users) can be self-directed as long as they have become committed to objectives they value. Working becomes as natural as eating or sleeping.

'Work is not the curse, but drudgery is', said Henry Ward Beecher in 1887. In more recent years, various research surveys conducted in Europe and the USA confirm that people would continue to work even if they did not need the money. Our own line management and consultancy careers have included thousands of interviews over many years with senior IT managers and consultants, all of whom confirm they are more interested in a challenging job than the amount of earnings. IT specialists and end-users place a higher value on the working environment, social and physical, than on the pay itself. Computer operations personnel associated with the large mainframe installations are becoming more motivated by the work they do, and less concerned with the complex structure of remuneration schemes associated with shift working. The higher value placed on work by many of today's IT labour force suggests that they may be more motivated to do their jobs, jobs which provide opportunities to develop their potential.

One of the tasks for executive management – those responsible for developing commercial, IT and HRM strategies – is to develop a corpo-rate environment in which jobs harness the positive motivational factors. It is only too easy to demotivate people, but implementing positive policies for motivation makes heavy demands on the skills and creative-ness of senior management. The jobs and conditions of work should promote self-motivation, and avoid dull and repetitive tasks. The need is for provision of opportunities for achievement, responsibility and creativity, whereby optimum utilization is made of talents, abilities and interests.

Theories of work motivation

Although there are many motivational theories, we will restrict ourselves to discussing four, the first two of which are similar, whilst the others view motivation from different perspectives. The examples we have selected are:

- Maslow's Hierarchy of Needs theory.[4, 5]
- Herzberg's Hygiene theory.[6]
- Adams's Equity theory.[7]
- Vroom, Lawler and Porter's Valence, Instrumentality, and Expectancy theory.[8, 9, 10]

Hierarchy of needs

Maslow suggests that human motivation is dependent on satisfying a hierarchical structure of needs. The needs dictate the way in which people behave and motivate themselves. The lower-order needs have to be satisfied before moving on to the higher-level needs. As each need is satisfied, the next need in the hierarchy is prompted. We list the five major categories in Figure 6.1, starting with the lowest level.

The basic needs are to satisfy the biological drives. The second level develops the need to be free from physical or psychological threats. The third level admits the needs of being loved and accepted by other people.

Figure 6.1 Hierarchy of needs.

Jointly, the first three levels are taken together as Group A and considered to be 'deficiency' needs. Maslow believed that if these needs were not met a person would fail to develop into a healthy person, both physically and psychologically.

Group B, the final two levels – esteem and self realization – are known as 'growth' needs. These requirements have to be gratified if a person is to grow or develop to their full potential.

The important point to remember with Maslow's hierarchy is that a person does not move on to the next level until all needs in previous levels have been satisfied. This means that management has to meet lower-order requirements and clear the way to the higher levels of self-actualization. The theory suggests that adequate salaries, company-wide social gatherings, and company awards, are supposed to lead on to maximum effective use of corporate human resources.

Practical application of the theory has led to some critical feedback. The levels do not always operate in the same sequence, and some researchers have failed to find confirmation of the five levels. For example, Alderfer[11] proposes a simplified hierarchy of needs (three levels), and states that these levels do not have to be activated in a specific order.

Although the specialists disagree amongst themselves about the exact number of levels and the relationships between the needs, the theory does have a contribution to make during the development of effective job motivation tactics for the IT environment.

Hygiene theory – taking the hierarchy of needs a stage further

Herzberg distinguished two categories of rewards, which can be related to Maslow's hierarchy of needs. First, rewards that satisfied lower order needs such as pay and working conditions were considered as parts of a hygiene factor. Any inadequacy in these rewards would create dissatisfaction, but adequate provision would not in turn generate motivation to perform the task better, or job satisfaction. Job satisfaction and job dissatisfaction, according to Herzberg, are therefore totally separate elements. Rewards such as achievement, responsibility, recognition and interesting work, which are addressed to Maslow's higher needs, were considered to form part of a motivating factor. Such rewards, Herzberg argued, will encourage commitment to high performance in the conduct of work as well as generate satisfaction.

Herzberg's theories have had considerable influence on job enrichment programmes but his methodology has been criticized, and other investigations have not supported his simple formula.

Equity theory

J. Stacy Adams, the originator of equity theory, suggests that workers are motivated to monitor and maintain the level of fair, or 'equitable', relationships between themselves and others, and change the unfair, or 'inequitable'. The theory proposes that workers make social comparisons between themselves and others in two areas:

- *Outcomes*, what they believe others and themselves receive from their jobs (pay, fringe benefits, and prestige);
- *Inputs*, what they believe others and themselves contribute to their jobs (amount of time worked, effort expended, and qualifications).

It is important to note our use of the word *believe* – the inputs and outcomes are as perceived by those involved in the work situation, not necessarily what they are in reality. Clearly, variances in perception can lead to much conflict and disagreement amongst workers, especially in the emerging end-user systems environment.

Outcomes and inputs are compared in the form of a ratio – the ratio of outcomes/inputs of work group 1 are compared to the ratio of outcomes/inputs of work group 2. These comparisons result in any one of three states: overpayment, underpayment, or equitable payment. Overpaid workers are supposed to feel guilty, underpaid workers are supposed to feel angry, whilst equitably paid workers are considered to be satisfied.

Equity theory suggests that workers are motivated to escape from the negative experience of anger and guilt. An end-user, developing and implementing systems on a PC, sees an IT specialist from the Information Centre doing very similar work but receiving a much higher salary. The end-user may consider redressing the inequity behaviourally by lowering his inputs (arriving late for work, leaving early, taking longer tea breaks, doing less work, or producing lower quality work). Alternatively, the end-user may show psychological responses – the situation may be thought about in a different way (the IT specialist really deserves such outcomes because of the number of end-users he/she supports) and the inequity is reduced.

The IT specialist may feel overpaid and raise the level of inputs, working harder and longer hours to support the Information Centre's objectives – to help end-users help themselves. Alternatively, the IT specialist may convince herself psychologically that she is worth the higher outcomes by virtue of superior knowledge gained over a longer period.

IT salaries move ahead far in excess of the national inflation rates, and IT specialists may rationalize these rises on the basis of higher value inputs, and that comparisons with other work groups do not constitute any form of inequity.

The perceptual nature of equity theory makes it possible for workers to disagree about what the inputs and outcomes may be in reality. There is much argument about 'comparable worth' and establishing the value of different job inputs so that pay equity can be established across the expanding IT environment.

A recent research study[12] examined the effects of adding additional responsibilities and high status job titles to workers' jobs. If extra responsibilities are given without increasing the outcome, there is an underpayment inequity. If we compensate the person for these added inputs, we produce an equitable state. To test the reasoning, students were hired to work in a group carrying out a task at a rate of pay they considered to be equitable. After an initial period, some of the students were singled out for good performance and given a 'senior' title. This required them to work longer hours to check other students' work. These senior members of the work group did not expect to be paid extra money for the work, they compensated by the status of the title. The performance of the first group was compared with a second work group, who likewise had some members selected to check the work of other students in their group. But those selected were not compensated with a high status job title, and they responded by lowering their inputs. Because management expected higher inputs, and made no adjustment to outputs (no senior title), the selected students reported feeling underpaid.

The feedback from practical application of the theory suggests that inequity not only motivates workers to escape inequitable situations, but concerns about equity also motivate some managers to attempt to create equitable relationships between themselves and their employees.

Valence-Instrumentality-Expectancy (VIE) theory

The first three theories we have discussed concentrated on individual needs and social comparisons. But we should consider the connections between motivation and the overall IT working environment. Pioneering work in this area was done by Vroom, Lawler and Porter in the middle to late 1960s. The results of their activities suggest that the relationship between behaviour and specified goals is not a simple matter.

Everybody has different goals, and people work towards those goals only if they feel there is a reasonable chance of their actions succeeding. VIE suggests that people are motivated to work when they expect to be able to achieve the results they want from their jobs. The theory is about viewing workers as rational beings who think about what actions they have to carry out to be rewarded, and how much the reward means to them before carrying out the tasks. But the theory does not stop at what people think, it makes links with other aspects of the environment which influence the task performance.

VIE theory suggests that motivation is the result of the interaction of three different types of understanding held by people in the work situation:

- *Expectation*, that effort will result in performance.
- *Instrumentality*, that performance will be rewarded.
- *Valence*, which is the perceived value of the rewards to the people receiving them.

In one circumstance, IT workers may believe that putting in a great deal of effort on a project will result in it being completed on time. But, on another occasion they may feel that however hard they work, they will not achieve the objective. High expectancy leads to more effort, low expectancy leads to less effort.

But working harder and achieving higher performance may be undermined if the company does not provide sufficient reward, if the higher performance is not perceived as being instrumental in bringing the IT workers a higher compensation. IT specialists and end-users may not be willing to put a great deal of extra effort into their respective aspects of a project if they perceive no one will notice or reward their effort.

If IT workers (managers, IT specialists, and end-users) receive compensation based on their performance, they will be poorly motivated if the rewards have a low value (valence) to them. Workers who do not care about the rewards given them by their company will not be motivated to attempt to attain them.

Vroom, Lawler and Porter claim that motivation, as described in VIE theory, is a combination of all three functions (valence, instrumentality, and expectancy). If all three functions are operating at high levels, then there will be high motivation. But should any one function be zero, then the overall level of motivation will be zero. A programmer who believes that his effort will result in high performance of a system, and that there will be appropriate reward, will have a motivation of zero if the valence (perceived value of the reward) is zero.

The logical flow of VIE theory is:

- Effort leads to performance which leads to reward.
- Effort and performance generate an expectancy.
- Performance and its link with reward creates the belief in instrumentality.
- Expectancy, instrumentality and valence of reward lead to motivation.
- Motivation interacting with the abilities and traits of the workers, together with their role perceptions and opportunities, leads to performance.

Skills and abilities are major contributors to an individual's task performance. Because of their unique qualities and special skills, some people are better for certain tasks. There are excellent programmers, and there are excellent systems analysts, but excellent systems analysts do not necessarily make excellent programmers or *vice versa*.

How a person's job is perceived by another worker will influence the performance of the individual. A senior systems analyst may believe that her primary job is to be responsible for the training of her team members. But if the systems and programming manager sees the senior systems analyst's job as being to keep the project moving, or ensuring systems development standard methods are used, he or she may be seen as a poor performer. The poor performance has nothing to do with lack of motivation, but a misunderstanding of the role to be played by the senior systems analyst.

If opportunities to perform well are limited, even the best workers will perform at low levels. A highly motivated programmer will perform badly if the availability of online terminals is denied during the crucial phases of developing online terminal systems.

There has been a mixed response to VIE theory, but some aspects have received much support, especially the links between expectancy and instrumentality and their impact on motivation.

The motivation of workers in the expanding IT environment will be improved if it can be seen that effort leads to performance. IT workers who receive training to do their jobs more effectively and efficiently will be more highly motivated and achieve higher levels of performance for their efforts. Managers should listen to the workers' suggestions for improving the structure of their jobs. IT workers are very aware of the problems in their jobs which interfere with performance. Making changes to working methods will allow for greater efficiency, and managers must ensure the desired performance is attainable. This aspect of VIE activities has strong connections with performance appraisal procedures.

All those working in the expanding IT environment should have a clear understanding of what is required of them, and the link between rewards and performance (instrumentality). Methods must be developed which link rewards more directly to IT performance.

These rewards will need to have a positive valence to IT workers. In the UK, the fall in the numbers of young people entering the IT labour market is a real challenge, but also the perceived values of rewards will be affected – what is of perceived value to a twenty-three year old IT worker may not have the same impact on a thirty-three year old IT worker. The demographic changes will demand reassessment of the perceived reward values. We see more need for 'menu-style' reward systems – incentive systems which allow IT workers to select their compensation package from a range of options (additional holidays, improved insurance benefits, more flexible working hours).

Turning motivation theory into practice

What sort of issues are raised for organizations by these theories when they are applied to motivation, rewards and incentives in the workplace?

On the one hand motivation is concerned with the satisfaction of needs. Should management therefore try to satisfy the needs of employees as a means of motivating them? Paternalistic styles of management are based on the idea that unconditional rewards across the board – pay, fringe benefits, recreational facilities, comfortable working conditions – will promote loyalty and productivity from the IT workforce. In fact satisfaction of such needs has not necessarily correlated with effective performance on a job, although people whose basic needs are satisfied appear less likely to leave than those whose basic needs are not satisfied.

The 'Needs' theories, be they Maslow or Herzberg, suggest that lower level needs are satisfied through economic rewards, higher level needs are satisfied through psychological and social rewards, and it is the satisfaction of higher needs that motivates people to do a job more effectively. Needs theories have directed management towards a greater awareness of motivators intrinsic to the job. This has resulted in job enrichment programmes, participative management styles, and achievement recognition. A further question arises. It may be desirable but is it possible to satisfy the higher needs of all employees in the IT workplace? Does this satisfaction depend on such social and cultural factors as the level of responsibility of the job, the type of worker and the nature of the work? The organizational development movement, fostering humanistic values in the organization, would say that it is both desirable and possible to satisfy higher needs in all employees who desire it, given a management attitude to people based on McGregor's *Theory Y*.

On the one hand, the Hawthorne studies have shown the important part esteem needs can play in motivation. No matter how bad working conditions were made for the girl assemblers, their output kept increasing because they felt special to the organization. On the other hand, J. H. Goldthorpe's studies[13] of affluent manual workers suggest that some workers do not expect to derive any satisfaction or self-fulfilment from their work. Work for them is just 'instrumental' in providing the means for self-fulfilment outside it. High wages are the motivation to increase their powers as consumers and their domestic standard of living.

Another question arises. Does the satisfaction of higher needs at work necessarily mean that more basic needs, for example pay, decline in importance to a person? The Needs theories' rigid distinction between hygiene factors and motivators has to be looked at carefully in the light of particular work group attitudes.

It is very difficult for management to base reward and incentive systems on the satisfaction of individual needs, because these are so variable between individuals or even within an individual at different times and in different circumstances.

It is perhaps easier for management therefore to look at the reward element in relation to individuals' behaviour when considering the best means of motivating their workforce.

Vroom's version of expectancy theory takes into account the importance of individual perceptions and attitudes in relation to performance rather than in relation to need, and the rewards of performance as a means of giving satisfaction. It is not enough to say that an outcome satisfies a need. The outcome has to be valued by the individual, and this individual must see him or herself as being able to achieve it. It is no use putting goals or rewards before IT people to promote their efforts if they do not value them or have no chance of attaining them. Attainment can depend on whether individual capabilities are developed by training and also on the attitude of management in fostering performance accomplishment.

Porter and Lawler took this further in showing that performance accomplishment, if recognized by appropriate extrinsic and intrinsic rewards, can result in satisfaction to the individual and reinforce the employee's effort to performance achievement. Taking this view, management would pursue a system of rewards and incentives linked to performance, a strategy with its roots in the scientific management methods of F. W. Taylor.

The Equity theory stresses that there is not one absolute reward level for given effort. Management has to pitch rewards and incentives at what employees regard as an equitable reward for effort in relation to their own expectations, which are in turn heavily influenced by the norms obtaining in their comparative reference group. Thus employers have also to take into account employee expectations and comparability in any design of reward and incentives packages.

The primary activity of managers, technical specialists and end-users, working in the IT environment is to make things happen. But this is not achieved just by implementing sophisticated hardware and software, all supported by complex planning activities. Making things happen is totally dependent upon our ability to work with and through other people. We all desire job satisfaction, and information technology is prompting us to respond to dramatically changing work situations. All corporate functions, working groups and individuals will have to come to terms with these challenges.

It is good commercial sense for companies to ask if they are allowing every member of their organizations to make optimum contribution to corporate success. Most of us realize it is far too easy to be demotivated by others, but too often we forget the negative impact of our own words and actions on other people in the organization. So what can be done?

Motivation through setting agreed performance requirements

There is a great deal of written material on the subject of setting and applying organizational goals. We have attempted to distil some of the main points, add our own experience and research, and identify those aspects we believe are linked with improving the motivation of those working within the ever expanding IT environment.[14]

The need is to set specific goals and not ask IT workers simply to do their best. The benefits of goals are long-lasting, but we do not under-estimate the difficulties in setting them.

The findings from a number of research studies[15] suggest that goals must be difficult, challenging and specific, if they are to raise performance. Specific and easy goals can lead to a lowering of performance. However, goals must not be too difficult or they will be rejected by IT workers. The unfortunate effects of setting too difficult goals was demonstrated in a recent study[16] of engineers performing a perceptual speed test requiring them to match the number of characters appearing in two lines of text. Performance levels improved with increasingly more difficult goals, but they only did so up to a point. As the goals became too difficult, the engineers rejected them and their performance dropped.

IT workers should be included in the goal-setting process because research findings indicate that people's performance is enhanced when they are involved. Those workers who accept goals prior to the goal-setting process do not demonstrate similar increases in performance.[17] Sometimes it is not practical to bring everyone into the detailed activities of setting goals. In these circumstances 'psychological contracts' – workers publicly committing themselves to achieving certain IT goals – have shown an increased acceptance of the given goals and the likelihood of them being reached.

The link between goal-setting and feedback is important. IT workers need to know how close they are to a performance goal in order to meet it. Research findings suggest it is not sufficient just to inform IT workers about the outcome of their efforts. There is a need to provide information about how and why certain actions have improved their performance. Gains in performance have connections with the level of information made available about the links between successful behaviour and performance.

We emphasize that goal-setting is not a simple matter. There are many problems which have to be solved or avoided. Quantified goal-setting is not easily implemented for all jobs in the IT environment. It may be possible to do so in the operational area and the systems development function (analysis and programming), but it becomes progressively more difficult in the higher levels of responsibility. Being objective in setting goals may be counterproductive if it diverts IT workers' attention away from the day-to-day targets.[18] Where an individual worker's performance is partially dependent upon the efforts of others (such as found in matrix-style IT project structures), it is questionable whether the individual's performance should be judged on the outcomes of the group. It is also quite difficult to assess the individual's contribution to the group's product – the final implemented system.

Goal-setting systems must not overburden managers with additional paperwork. Managers under such pressures sometimes attempt to force IT workers to accept goals – this completely undermines the effectiveness of goal-setting. A research study in the USA of two hundred senior managers found that sixty-four per cent agreed with the statement 'managers today feel under pressure to compromise personal standards to achieve company goals'.[19] It seems that personal ethics are being sacrificed in the name of goal attainment, but so too are organizational ethics, with many companies falsifying records to appear to meet organizational goals.[20]

The basic message from all the research into practical examples of goal-setting is clear. The technique should be applied only to those areas of the IT environment where it is possible to produce meaningful goals. The importance and need for goals must be treated with common sense, and the development of dangerous tactical short-cuts avoided.

Motivation through job design, task restructuring, and job enrichment

We discuss the productivity aspects of the evolving IT environment in the next chapter, but motivation theories and their practical implementation require mention be made of job design, task restructuring and job enrichment, all of which can lead to improved performance.

Job design, task restructuring and job enrichment will be of increasing importance during the development and implementation of end-user systems. We believe there is sufficient evidence to prove the existence of very strong links between the shape and content of an IT job and the motivation of its incumbent.

All jobs should be extrinsically and intrinsically rewarding. Pay and fringe benefits derive from doing the job rather than the work itself. Feelings of accomplishment and personal growth are directly linked with the tasks which make up the job.

One of the early ways used to motivate personnel in the industrial production environment was to expand the content of the job, in other words increase the number of tasks. The worker performed a wider range of tasks, but the tasks were on all the same level – the restructuring (or job enlargement) had led to an increase in the horizontal task components of the job. This resulted in much criticism because the restructuring had resulted in multiples of the original task(s). Herzberg made the cynical comment that job enlargement had merely added to the meaninglessness of many jobs.

In the end-user systems environment, people are given the opportunity to have greater responsibility for their IT work and take greater control over how they perform the various tasks which make up the jobs. Providing these end-user systems are structured correctly, people will have increased opportunities for performing work at higher levels – the design (or job enrichment) has led to an increase in the vertical task components of the job.

In 1968, Herzberg redesigned the jobs of a group of stock holder correspondents. The redesigned jobs gave greater responsibility and sense of achievement. A control group was set up and monitored in order to identify any changes due to the 'Hawthorne' effect. After the first three months the performance of those in the job enrichment group fell below those in the control group, but six months later their performance was significantly higher. The attitudes towards tasks were also measured in each group – the attitudes of the job enrichment group were clearly more positive.[21]

Job enrichment projects have been subjected to considerable research and investigation which has resulted in the identification of various difficulties. Implementation problems come high on the list of criticisms, seemingly because of the expense associated with redesigning existing physical plant. Technology already used in existing tasks was considered to reduce the number of options for job enrichment – research in the USA suggests that technology and its management are inflexible.

Workers do not always want the added responsibility which accompanies job enrichment. It seems enriched jobs are not for everybody, although workers who feel the need to achieve – those who could be described as strivers – welcome the possibility of job enrichment.

Several problems present themselves when considering job enrichment for the IT environment. Certain elements of jobs need to be enriched because they alter workers' psychological views about their work. But which elements of the jobs need to be enriched to make them more effective, and how can the requirements be specified?

Research in the USA, conducted by Hackman and Oldman,[22] suggests there are five core job dimensions that create three critical psychological states which in turn lead to several beneficial outcomes for workers and their organizations – see Figure 6.2.

Skill variety is concerned with the way in which a job utilizes a worker's different skills and abilities. *Task identity* is about the extent to which a job requires the completion of a whole piece of work from beginning to end. *Task significance* is the degree of impact a job is believed to have on other people. When these dimensions of a job are balanced satisfactorily, they should lead to the job being experienced as meaningful.

Autonomy is the level of freedom and discretion a worker has to carry

Core job dimensions:	Psychological states:	Beneficial outcomes:
Skill variety, Task identity, Task significance.	Experienced meaningfulness at work.	High internal motivation. High quality work performance.
Autonomy	Experienced responsibility for outcomes of the work.	High satisfaction with the work.
Feedback	Knowledge of the actual results of the work activities	Low absenteeism and turnover.

Figure 6.2 Dimensions of jobs and how they can be enriched

out the job as desired. As in the end-user systems environment, autonomous jobs allow workers to feel personally responsible and accountable for the IT work they perform.

Feedback allows the workers to have information about the effects of their work, and allows them to tune finely their performance.

The research findings suggest that the three critical psychological states influence workers' feelings of motivation, the quality of work performed, satisfaction with work, and absenteeism and turnover.

Jobs may have to be redistributed so that an individual worker may take credit for it (task identity and task significance). Tasks may have to be combined to enable workers to perform the entire job (skill variety, task identity). Workers may have to establish contact with clients of their services and ultimate users of their products (autonomy and feedback). Information channels may have to be opened to give workers knowledge of the results of their work (feedback).

We emphasize that implementing job enrichment programmes is not easy, but the job and role challenges of the emerging information technology environment suggest the approach will become increasingly more important.

The real challenges

The right combinations of aptitudes and attitudes

To be successful in almost any IT job during the late 1990s will require a combination of several aptitudes and the changing of attitudes. There are many ways in which aptitudes can be assessed and they are well documented. These methods allow for objectively understanding intellectual strengths and weaknesses, together with identifying specific skills. But we believe the need for changing of attitudes should be high on the list of priority tasks for commercial, IT, and HRM management. Identification of appropriate aptitudes does not guarantee that people will be successful in a particular activity. Many other factors, such as motivation, self-image, attitudes, and anxiety, will influence attainment.

Response to change

Change is an inherent part of our lives, and it will become even more so as we move towards the close of this century. We all resist change – why? Are we resisting the changes themselves, or the fact that we have to adapt to the new circumstances? Many of the developments emerging from information technology will bring benefits to companies and individuals. But people have fears about loss of job and earnings, demands for new skills, and the threat of changes in relationships. We all have moments of panic when we wonder whether we will be able to adapt to the changes.

Introducing new technology, changing remuneration packages, or integrating several commercial operations into one are seen to be major changes. Modifying the layout of the reception area, changing the time of tea breaks, or reorganizing the corporate car park layout are often seen to be minor changes. But minor changes can have major consequences: one person's minor change is another's major change – a point always to remember in the evolving IT environment.

Quality of leadership

During the final decade of the 1990s, senior executive management, more than ever before, will be expected to provide inspirational leadership which promotes confidence, projects an optimistic image, 'walks' the job and is seen, generates new ideas, capitalizes on change, has the moral courage to take the right decisions, communicates constantly, recognizes and deals with stress in themselves and others, enthuses people and, if at all possible, maintains a sense of humour.

IT managers, together with their commercial and HRM colleagues, will not only need to understand their own jobs and perform them well, but have an adequate understanding of other management disciplines. They will be required to define exactly what is expected of their staff, never let them down, and enjoy working with them.

Successful implementation of information technology is closely linked with how motivation activities are handled. Creating a good working atmosphere, and drawing people together as effective teams, are continual requirements.

Can the classical motivation theories deliver the goods?

But will the classical motivation theories and associated techniques alone adequately support the commercial/IT/HRM strategies of the 1990s? We believe they will not. Our concern is caused by the level and pace of change associated with information technology. Future career choices and requirements for new skills in the rapidly changing IT environment will demand that more emphasis is placed on understanding who a person really is – the identification of each person's 'basic design'.

Although people are adaptable, the new roles are stressing different sets of aptitudes and attitudes for technical and commercial personnel. Motivation 'profiles' will have to be developed for each employee which relate the individual's range of aptitudes and attitudes to the requirements of the new roles.

Our line management and consultancy experience confirms that the need to change, to take on new concepts and even abandon technologies acclaimed only months before, is part of most IT careers. The changes are often fundamental yet not always recognized as such. IT specialists and end-users are expected to be flexible and to adapt. As we said at the beginning of this chapter, there is a failure to recognize that whilst there is great capacity to adapt within an individual's life script, they may in their current role be operating at the extremes. Further pressure to bend in a particular direction may take them far from their own natural pattern with disastrous consequences. There are costly penalties to be paid for not checking whether the elements of the jobs evolving in the IT environment match with the characteristics of individuals already in jobs or situations where their motivation has led them to being successful.

Personal success in every situation?

We are not advocating a Machiavellian concept which allows senior executive management to manipulate the organization by the means of an on/off motivational switch! On the contrary, the need is to help members of organizations help themselves when facing the motivational challenges of the information technology environment. Each person's personality, character, and talents have done much to shape the important events in their lives (business and private). There is a clear, strong connection between who a person is and what they have done. Individual design, or makeup, is a strong driving force. We believe 'motivational patterning' as identified by Arthur F. Miller and Ralph T. Mattson in their research and consulting activities[23] will be a major component in human resource management strategies for all personnel associated with IT.

Miller and Mattson suggest that job mismatch reveals itself in familiar attitudes: petulance, sullenness, unresponsiveness, lack of alertness or initiative, and unthinking indifference. Regardless of level or function, when work does not engage employee strengths the employer reaps a litany of problems: productivity problems, emotional problems, morale problems, loyalty problems, conflict problems, and troublemaker problems'.[24]

All these negative attitudes and problems which accompany a mismatch between the individual and the job are accompanied by a great deal of internal stress within the person. Evidence is growing to support the view that job mismatch is contributing to heart ailments, marital problems, alcoholism, drug addiction, mental and emotional disorder, disability and even early death. Given the changes of roles and jobs suggested by evolving IT, we see major problems ahead unless managers recognize this situation and take effective action.

Normally, in an external recruitment or internal promotion situation, specifications will exist for the job and person required. Often the decisions are made on information about past and present performance. This can lead to falling into the 'Peter trap' – current performance good, therefore performance in the new job will be good – and the recruitment or promotion results in people being placed into positions beyond their competence.

Miller suggests that unreliable data is the curse to be avoided. He quotes examples of illogical conclusions based on the courses a person studied at college or university – education never creates a new strength, it only exercises and gives a vocabulary to develop that which already exists. Grades received or type and lengths of education are all suspect data; they may or may not reveal a strength and should be weighted, because they do not correlate to success in the world of work.

Because of all these difficulties with basic data and its interpretation, organizations jump into psychological testing and believe that they have produced 'profiles' able to predict the future performance of potential candidates. The testing assists in the identification of particular skills or capabilities which have been defined as necessary for success in the role or job, but they do not identify motivation.

The methods and procedures which have been developed by Miller and Mattson, known as SIMA (System for Identifying Motivated Abilities), are based on the premise that from early childhood each one of us reveals that we are good at, and motivated to do, certain things for certain purposes. There is no outstanding performance, no innovation, no major improvement, no bright new idea, no important product development, no well-conceived strategy, no sound business decision, no big sale – unless and until these strengths are brought into action. The presence or absence of these strengths are critical to job success or failure. In outline, the SIMA process[25] consists of eliciting from people their recollection of past enjoyable achievement experiences – school, home, work, recreation, and in normal and abnormal circumstances. The person is encouraged to describe in exhaustive detail how they went about doing what they did. Holding together the entire system of identifying motivated behaviour is a phenomenon that a person will repeat some or all of the same elements of a previous task which he or she perceived as satisfying and well done. This behaviour can be described in common behavioural terms – see Figure 6.3. The behavioural actions are in response to expressed needs, within a changing, fluid set of circumstances, which achieved measurable results.

All this is captured on audio/video tape and usually reduced to a typed transcript, collating what was written and said. Recurring threads and themes are then gathered together into what is known as a motivational pattern. The pattern consists of:

- A central motivational thrust (to be the best, overcome obstacles, serve others, acquire money/materials/status, exploit potential, pioneer/explore, etc.).
- Abilities which the person is motivated to use (to schedule, design, persuade, experiment, organize, analyse, write, conceive ideas).
- Subject matter which the person is motivated to work with (tangible, intangible, data, technical, people).
- Circumstances within which the person is motivated to work (amount or absence of structure, visibility factors, working conditions, nature of environment/organization).
- Relations which the person is motivated to establish with others (individualist, team member, coach, director, manager, dependent on authority, independent).

The components of the motivation are gathered together to describe and predict how the achiever would attempt any job.

The motivational pattern represents the essence of the person: they will try to perform work in accordance with their motivational pattern. For example an *innovator* will change things, an *overcomer* will find or

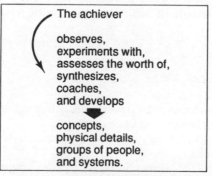

Figure 6.3 The behavioural phenomenon underlying SIMA

make things to overcome, a *doer* will continue to perform the details – regardless of what is wanted, expected or necessary. A person's motivational pattern is never satiated, regardless of how many satisfying achievements he or she has experienced. The child concerned with acquiring money at the age of seven is still concerned with acquiring money half a century later, regardless of how much has been acquired. The motivational pattern emerges early and remains constant.

In summary, motivational patterning allows for more effective decisions about current and future job decisions in terms of lessening misfit, and improving productivity and employee satisfaction. If performance starts to go sour in the IT function, or in an end-user systems environment, look for recent changes in supervision, policies or strategies, working location or conditions which may have altered some previously matching quality; suspect the seeds of incompatibility, and examine the employee's strength against the new mix of job requirements.

The simple message from motivational patterning is that job misfit corrupts and destroys people and organizations. Assuring role or job fit in the emerging IT environment by identifying, developing and making productive use of employee strengths will make a large and sustained contribution to the profitability of the organization, and to the quality of life experienced by commercial/IT managers, technical specialists and end-users.

An environment in which people can develop

If you have stayed with us to this point, you will have recognized that motivation is a highly complex and contentious area of human experience. Whilst motivation is facilitated by a variety of external factors – remuneration, terms and conditions of employment, recognition, responsibility, and challenging work – their interaction takes place within each individual. How each person responds is completely dependent upon his or her unique motivational pattern. Management's role is to create an appropriate environment in which people will grow and give of their best.

Notes and references

1   Robert A. Baron , *Behaviour in Organizations: Understanding and Managing the Human Side of Work* (Allyn and Bacon, 1986).
2   M. London, 'Towards a theory of career motivation', *Academy of Management Review*, 8, pp. 620-630.
3   Douglas McGregor, *The Human Side of Enterprise* (Penguin Books, 1987).
4   A. H. Maslow, *Motivation and Personality* (Harper and Row, 1970).

5   H. S. Schwartz, 'Maslow and the hierarchical enactment of organizational reality', *Human Relations*, **36**, pp. 933-956, 1983.
6   F. Herzberg, *Work and the Nature of Man* (World Publishing, 1966).
7   J. S. Adams, 'Inequity in social exchange' in *Advances in Experimental Psychology*, ed. L. Berkowitz, Vol 2 (Academic Press, 1965).
8   V. H. Vroom, *Work and Motivation* (John Wiley, 1964).
9   E. E. Lawler and L. W. Porter, 'Antecedent attitudes of effective managerial performance' in *Organizational Behaviour*, Vol 2, pp. 122-142, 1967.
10 E. E. Lawler and L. W. Porter, *Managerial Attitudes and Performance* (Irwin Dorsey, 1968).
11 C. P. Alderfer, 'An empirical test of a new theory of human needs', *Organisational Behaviour and Human Performance*, **4**, pp. 142-175, 1969.
12 J. Greenberg and S. Ornstein, 'High status job title as compensation for underpayment: a test of equity theory', *Journal of Applied Psychology*, **68**, pp. 285-297, 1983.
13 J. H. Goldthorpe *et al.*, *The Affluent Worker: Industrial Attitudes and Behaviour* (Cambridge University Press, 1968).
14 E. A. Lock and G. P. Latham, *Goal-setting: A Motivational Technique That Works!* (Prentice Hall, 1984).
15 L. Miller, *Behaviour Management: The New Science of Managing People at Work* (John Wiley, 1978).
16 M. Erez and I. Zidon, 'Effect of goal acceptance on the relationship of goal difficulty to performance', *Journal of Applied Psychology*, **69**, pp. 69-78, 1984.
17 M. Erez and F. H. Kanfer, 'The role of goal acceptance in goal setting and task performance', *Academy of Managment Review*, **8**, pp. 454-463, 1983.
18 C. I. Stein, 'Objective management systems: two to five years after implementation', *Personnel Journal*, **54**, pp. 525-528, 1979.
19 A. B. Carroll, 'Managerial ethics: a post-Watergate review', *Business Horizons*, **18 (2)**, pp. 75-80, 1975.
20 G. Getschow, 'Some middle managers cut corners to achieve high corporate goals', *Wall Street Journal*, November 8, pp. 1 and 26, 1979.
21 D. Torrington and L. Hall, *Personnel Management – A New Approach*, pp. 362-363 (Prentice Hall, 1987).
22 J. R. Hackman and G. R. Oldham, *Work Redesign* (Addison-Wesley, 1980).
23 Arthur F. Miller and Ralph T. Mattson, *The Truth About You* (Fleming H. Revel Company, 1977).
24 Arthur F. Miller, 'Identifying motivation to minimize mismatch', *Personnel Management*, October 1985 (Institute of Personnel Management).
25 SIMA procedures are the copyright property of People Management Inc., Simsbury, Connecticut, USA.

CHAPTER 7

IMPROVED UTILIZATION OF HUMAN RESOURCES – YES, BUT HOW?

Many companies are continuing to experience problems with maintaining ageing information systems based on mainframe computers. In addition, the emergence of personal computers (PCs) and end-user systems is revealing a hidden backlog of systems requirements. A significant number of IT human resources are tied up with supporting and amending monolithic applications inherited from the early 1970s. These applications have survived transfer from one generation of hardware to another, operate in ever more sophisticated technical environments, and remain a maintenance nightmare for systems development personnel, often leading to a high labour turnover of IT specialists.

Measuring the productivity of IT is not easy. The work processes are complex, and a clearly definable unit of output against which IT manpower costs can be compared is the subject of much debate. Often the measurements are used to focus on improving the efficiency of detailed IT operations, rather than on increasing the effectiveness and added value of information systems.

Although more organizations are introducing performance appraisal, the corporate changes implied in information technology strategies for the 1990s suggest that there is an urgent need to develop effective procedures for informing people of exactly what is expected of them, how they are to be measured, and how they are progressing.

Because of the need to respond to shorter project timescales for developing and maintaining information systems, a wide variety of productivity improvement tools have been introduced to the IT environment – all are ways of improving the production of program coding, and developing system specifications. Most of these tools are provided for IT specialists. What evidence is there to suggest that there are tools which will help end-users to help themselves?

Our approach to improving the utilization and productivity of IT human resources (managers, specialists and end-users) is not to direct attention to establishing detailed measurements for specific activities. We believe the fundamental improvements will be achieved more readily by implementing personnel appraisal methods, understanding the dynamics of work groups, developing structured decision-making, facilitating improved personal communication, and effective use of computer-assisted systems engineering.

Job satisfaction and performance

Can it be taken for granted that workers experiencing job satisfaction in the IT environment are more productive workers? Will end-users who develop and implement their own information systems be more productive than those who are unhappy and dissatisfied with systems based on central computing facilities? Is an IT specialist, who is experiencing job satisfaction in an Information Centre environment, more productive than a frustrated IT specialist working in a corporate data centre supporting ageing application systems? To answer these questions requires an understanding of job satisfaction and performance.

Is there a direct link between job satisfaction and performance?

Research suggests that the connection between job satisfaction and performance is tenuous.[1] Performance does not rise in response to increased job satisfaction. Why is this the case?

In many IT work settings, as currently structured, there is little room for individuals to improve their performance. The jobs are designed so that the incumbents achieve at least some minimum level of attainment – if they do not, they find themselves out of a job! In addition, no allowance is made for exceeding this basic level of performance. For example, a systems analyst working in a project team, which is organized along matrix lines, may wish to improve his or her performance, but this will be to little purpose if other members of the team continue to work at the previous pace, because activities in project teams are often highly inter-related. Programmers attempting to develop systems using on-line terminals may be frustrated by the amount of machine time made available for testing their programs. High levels of job satisfaction would not lead to higher performance of the human resources in either example.

As suggested in Chapter 6, levels of performance lead to extrinsic and intrinsic rewards (pay, and the feeling of achievement). If these rewards are judged to be fair by IT personnel, they may come to see a dependent relationship between their performance and these outcomes. It may encourage high levels of effort and good performance. It may lead to job satisfaction. But the two factors are not directly linked.[2]

What behaviour is influenced by job satisfaction?

Job satisfaction influences absenteeism and turnover, but is not directly related to standard measures of job performance. There is some evidence that job satisfaction can lead people to facilitate a smoother operation of their organizations, but this is not to say that their individual performance has improved. Research in the USA suggests that when workers experience positive feelings, they are more likely to be helpful than when they have negative feelings. But output and quality indices do not possess a strong link with job satisfaction.[3]

Effective appraisal can lead to improved utilization

Management spends a great deal of its time monitoring investments in buildings, equipment and services. However, our own research studies suggest that appraisal of the IT human resource investments (managers, specialists and end-users), in terms of performance against results, is not carried out with the same objectivity.

Even in those companies where appraisal procedures are in operation, there is no guarantee the performance of IT human resources is subject to effective review. In our sample, one-third of the organizations confirmed that IT personnel are appraised, one-third stated the IT human resources are not taken into account, and one-third admitted no form of performance appraisal being used in their companies. Although other research studies[4] suggest that there is a growing attention to performance appraisal procedures within organizations and an increasing number are introducing appraisal at all organizational levels, the approach appears to be having minimum impact within the IT environment.

The need for effective performance appraisal

People in an organization need to know what is expected of them, how they are going to be measured, and most importantly how they are progressing. Otherwise they become frustrated and perform poorly.

But given the results of our own research surveys, why are so many IT managers and their colleagues negative in their response to performance appraisal? There is much misunderstanding. Many executives do not know how to go about setting up standards of performance for IT personnel. There is confusion about what job elements are or are not within an individual's control. Those responsible for the appraisals frequently dislike being part of the feedback process. Ineffective handling of appraisal procedures can lead to a build-up of suspicion amongst IT workers. Inappropriate subjective measurements can destroy motivation, and people fear being appraised on personality traits rather than results.

Performance appraisal can be negative

Much damage has been done to the concept of performance appraisal by formalized schemes which suggest everyone should be appraised once a year. The time for appraisal is greeted with as much enthusiasm as the yearly dose of influenza! The principal reasons given for carrying out appraisals of this type are the needs to evaluate each individual in terms of salary, promotion or career development. These schemes tend to concentrate on evaluating personal characteristics instead of focusing on the value added by each individual during the process of carrying out their work. Managers and supervisors are faced with completing multi-page documents which purport to assist in the appraisal of each individual reporting to them. Long lists of ambiguous terms are provided to describe aspects of personality – most of which can only be judged subjectively! The person being appraised sees the whole process as a personal attack and moves into a defensive stance. Instead of appraisal being a means of giving positive guidance, it becomes reduced to a *pat on the head* or *pull your finger out* session. Appraisal becomes the yearly 'spring clean', a time for everyone to fear, a time for making bookings on the redundancy bus or seriously looking at the job advertisements. Reward and punishment schemes not only undermine the value-added activities of those being appraised, but they can generate negative pressure on the managers and supervisors carrying out the appraisals.

The benefits of a positive approach to performance appraisal

The objectives of an appraisal should be to improve the abilities of the individual for increasing value-added performance, identify any obstacles which restrict this improvement, and agree a plan for achieving the projected improvement. It is imperative that this is done through the joint setting of objectives.

It is important to realize that the effectiveness of appraisal is totally dependent upon the skills of the appraiser. The procedures can help or hinder in the process, but the primary factor is the professional ability of the managers and supervisors carrying out the appraisal.

There are many benefits for the appraising manager/supervisor and the person being appraised: improved performance of individuals and departments, better communication, more effective relationships, identification of strengths and weaknesses, discovery of existing and potential problems, identification of training and development needs, clarification of jobs and roles, and increased opportunities to express views. The organization receives a wide range of benefits including improved value-added performance of individuals and departments, improved quality, and better understanding of labour turnover, all of which lead to improved profitability.

Successful appraisal requires realistic performance standards

Effective performance appraisal, especially for the information technology environment, requires a common understanding of the performance standard required from each person. This is a complex task, which most managers would prefer to avoid. Some IT functions resist any attempt to define standards of performance because they may impose restrictions on flexibility of working methods. We agree a level of controlled flexibility is essential, but unmanaged flexibility will lead to ineffective utilization of the human resources. It is no good complaining about skill shortages if no attempt is made to improve the utilization of existing IT personnel, and this will be dependent on the existence of realistic performance standards.

But recognizing the needs for effective performance standards is one thing, knowing how to go about setting them up is another.

Each job has to be looked at in its totality. Some parts of a job are vital to the process of creating value-added IT, and it is these which must have appropriate performance standards. A common response from managers, when faced with identifying the crucial value-added elements in each job, is to say they will not have any time to manage! But the essence of management is about identifying the value-added aspects and facilitating ever higher performance.

Setting effective performance standards

The keys to successful standards are the identification of appropriate criteria and the availability of information describing the performance. Management must give careful thought to how information about performance is to be collected. Many a good intention has collapsed into confusion because of the data collection problems. For example, we know of one IT function where a large proportion of the staff were spending the whole of every Friday afternoon each week filling in complex documents which collected data about their performance in the previous four and a half days – ten per cent of each working week was given over to collecting data, all at a time when there were severe skill shortages leading to problems with projects, and extensive requirements for overtime working! We are pleased to say a more acceptable way of monitoring performance has since been introduced.

The rules for setting standards are quite simple. The detailed activities are more complex, but the essence of successful implementation is contained in the four words validity, agreement, realism, and objectivity:[5]

- *Validity*: the standard must be valid in terms of the value-added component. For example, in some situations dress is very important. Many end-users of central computing facilities may believe untidy dressing habits of analysts and programmers suggest a 'slap happy' attitude to the quality of the product(s) and services. In other situations, standard of dress could be an irrelevant element, because there is no link with value-added.
- *Agreement*: standards should not be imposed, they should be mutually agreed. If a standard is imposed, then everyone runs to look for reasons why the standard cannot be achieved. When a standard is agreed, everyone attempts to overcome difficulties should they arise.
- *Realism*: a standard must be realistic. There is little point in striving for perfection if this cannot be achieved. It is not realistic to tell a project manager he or she must implement an IT application in half the time requested during a period of high labour turnover of team members. The balance has to be between too low standards, which do not extend, and too high standards which result in demotivating the individual.
- *Objectivity*: there must be objective measures to assess or appraise performance. The absence of objective measures means that performance can only be judged subjectively – which will lead to much conflict and a reduction in the value-added component.

Will performance appraisal be effective in any corporate culture?

Performance appraisal should not be seen as an approach which can be imported into any organization to overcome all the performance challenges associated with human resources working in the IT environment of the 1990s. It makes demands on the corporate culture. There are problems if the approach is brought into companies which are 'tone deaf' to effective human resource management. As we stated in Chapter 4, the nature of an organization's culture is a key factor. Corporate cultures are made up of sub-cultures where a wide variety of tribal rites and languages may exist. Participative goal setting may be acceptable to the IT function, but the financial or production areas – which may be the end-users of computing facilities – might be highly autocratic and hierarchical sub-cultures. It may be the reverse, with IT wearing the hard-nosed hat and end-user functions demonstrating flexibility.

Appraisers and appraisees should be trained in the appraisal process, the techniques and the difficulties. Whilst training of appraisers is accepted, training of appraisees raises some eyebrows. Appraisees should not be left to experience the process, something which is done to them. They should be part of the development and implementation of the 'life style'.

We believe that performance appraisal has a major role to play in any attempt to establish an effective human resource management strategy for the evolving information technology environment. But we emphasize that appraisal should not be seen as an HRM plaything, another technique brought in and handled by specialists. Appraisal must be part of the day-to-day interactions within a business, not a yearly event which expects everyone to do penance as part of the performance stocktaking.

Work groups and the information technology environment

One common factor linking human resource management strategies for the various information technology environments of the 1990s – centralized, distributed, or end-user computing – is group dynamics. Managers need to understand the nature and operation of work groups if companies are to gain the full benefits of IT.

What is a group?

A group is more than a random collection of people. Individuals have to interact verbally, for example sharing plans during a project meeting. There are non-verbal interactions such as smiles or angry looks, silent expressions of success or failure. People have to be able to influence each other to be seen as a group. We would not consider five systems analysts developing five independent applications, working in five separate locations and incapable of influencing each other, to be a group. There has to be some form of structure which allows for stable relationships between members. The members have to share common goals which could not be achieved as individual work units, and they must be able to perceive themselves as a group.

Group behaviour

We have not attempted to distil the received wisdom of all the contributions made by the social scientists about group behaviour, since to do so would be an occupation for a lifetime. Instead, we have taken our line management and consultancy experience, the results of our research, and added some aspects of behavioural science.

To be effective, IT groups must have a stable structure. This structure is mainly concerned with the relationships between those who make up the group. To understand relationships in groups, we have to be aware of three basic concepts: cohesiveness, norms, and roles.

Cohesiveness, or 'stickability', describes the quality of the group in terms of its members' likes and dislikes of each other. IT work groups with high cohesiveness are more likely to succeed than those with low cohesiveness. But work groups with low cohesiveness do not necessarily fail in their tasks – there could be a great deal of working at cross-purposes to achieve the goals, but the project is completed on time and within the financial budget. Work groups with a high level of cohesiveness does not guarantee a successful project – the members of the group may be caught up in 'groupthink', which can result in poor quality decisions and a failure to reach the defined goals.[6]

The cohesiveness of an IT work group can influence its productivity in many ways. When a project is completed successfully, the group members may recognize that they have worked well together. But because members of a work group or project team have a high level of cohesiveness, it does not mean that they will perform well within the overall context of either the IT function or the corporate organization. The work group may have internalized their own set of objectives which are totally at variance with the requirements of the surrounding organization. There are examples of highly cohesive project teams which have actively set out to undermine agreed strategic plans. The lesson to learn from high cohesiveness is that it can aid productivity, providing that the work group members and the surrounding management structure are not working in opposition to each other.

Within a work group there are rules which govern the behaviour of the members. These rules are called 'norms', but it is important to realize that they are not written or formal. The norms may dictate behaviour, or dictate behaviour which should be avoided. The prescriptive norms may dictate the relationship with the work group's leader, how a particular level of performance should be reached, or whether to help a fellow work group member who is in trouble with a particular aspect of the project, whereas the proscriptive norms may dictate that no member of the work group may work longer hours than the other members.

The norms may have developed over a period of time, especially if the work group continues to work over several years as a single unit on different applications, rather than being disbanded on completion of a project. Norms can be transferred in from other work groups – members drawing on their previous experiences to guide them in their behaviour in the new group. Having to learn fewer norms can lead to more effective social interaction within the work group.

We discussed the concept of roles in Chapter 4, but there are certain aspects which need emphasizing in terms of their effect on utilization and productivity. Within any work group its members, irrespective of their job titles and descriptions, play various roles in the group's interaction. A role suggests a range of behaviour expected from the person playing the role (the role incumbent). Each role player is required to recognize the behaviour expected of him or her – given effective role recognition there will be less social disorganization within the work group.

Role differentiation has to be considered carefully when building a work group, because work group members play different roles (task-specialist and socio-emotional). The mix of roles can facilitate the success of a work group, or destroy it. Senior managers responsible for setting up a project team must realize that work group structuring for a series of tasks requires more than just locating a project leader and the appropriate number of application/technical specialists. These work group members will adopt roles, but the roles do not automatically emerge from the project itself; they are dependent on the individuals and their interaction with each other.

The dynamics of the roles may lead to much internal stress for each individual and to conflict within the work group. Role conflict promotes job dissatisfaction, poor performance of individuals, and rejection of group members – all of which lead to a lowering in performance and disastrous consequences for IT strategies.

Group tasks

An IT work group performs a wide range of commercial and technical tasks during the life of a development project. Some of these tasks are extremely complex, and they are structured into smaller sub-tasks. A member of a work group may perform one single task, or be involved in a range of sub-tasks. Given the number of tasks carried out within a work group, how can they be combined to form a work group product?

Several general terms are used to describe the different types of task carried out by a work group: additive, compensatory, disjunctive, and conjunctive. Where the individual contributions of several members are combined and taken as the work group's product, they are called 'additive' tasks. For example, a project might require the analysis of data terms used by several end-users in a particular commercial application.

The analysis may be carried out by several systems analysts in the work group. The results of their study would be brought together to yield the product of their task. The task was dependent on each member's efforts – the more diligent each person is in their search for data definitions, the higher will be the group's output.

The work group may have to reassess the time and cost elements for their project. Each member will produce his or her own assessments which in turn have to be discussed and evaluated amongst the group. The final assessment will be based upon the average judgment of all the work group members – this type of activity is called a 'compensatory' task.

A project may reach a point where the level of troubles suggests a meeting of the work group to discuss what needs to be done. The discussions may result in members identifying two different approaches for overcoming the various problems identified, each approach having its own supporters. The work group has to make a choice between the two approaches. It is an 'either-or' situation. Only one of the approaches can be the workgroup's product, the other will be discarded. A task of this type is called 'disjunctive'.

On another occasion the work group may review its project, and recognize that its progress is dictated by the performance and abilities of its weakest members. The work group has a 'conjunctive' task – all members must work in unison and progress is dependent upon the slowest.

The concept of these different task-types has several implications for the utilization and productivity of IT human resources. During additive tasks, where individual contributions are added together, work group members do not always work as hard as they do as individuals – the 'social loafing' syndrome raises its head. Too many people working on a task can lead to a lowering in the productivity of the work group – individual members can lose themselves in the crowd. The solution to this problem is to make each individual's performance identifiable (a relay race will produce better individual performances than a mass marathon).

When all the members of an IT work group are expected to assess the time required for achieving a specific project goal, there will be a variety of forecasts produced. Some will be too high, others will be too low, and a compromise has to be reached. The correct assessment is more likely to be the average of the decisions, rather than an individual forecast. Research studies have found that compensatory task activities tend to make more accurate judgments than those of many individual work group members.[7]

There are circumstances where work group members cannot compromise but have to make a choice between two options – a disjunctive task. It is not surprising that the odds for coming up with the right answer are more favourable in larger work groups. But the right solution is not necessarily recognized as correct by work group members. Some solutions to project problems are obviously correct – often referred to as the 'eureka' tasks! But many solutions have to be sold to other members of the work group before gaining acceptance – it is not enough just to have a correct solution, the support of other members for the solution has to be gained.

IT work groups are always under pressure to ensure the project is completed on time and within the financial budgets. Therefore, work groups cannot afford to be slowed down to the pace of the least effective member. If after several attempts to help the person, the work group continues to be held back, there will be growing social pressure for the person to resign or be dismissed as incompetent.

In summary, during additive tasks work groups may be expected to perform better than individual members, although on conjunctive tasks the average member would out-perform the group. But during additive tasks there may be the problem of social loafing. In a disjunctive task situation, the quality of a work group's decision will be dependent upon the group's willingness to accept the solution proposed.

Leadership can be creative or the source of much demotivation

Leadership in the IT environment is a crucial issue. We have seen a variety of leadership styles in our line management and consulting careers. Our research activities for this book brought us into contact with a wide range of managers, some battling to keep the IT boat afloat, and others who seemed to have everything under control. The successful and not so successful managers (dare we say failures?) possessed widely differing management styles. Some of the IT functions were populated by highly motivated and very creative people, whilst others were dreary prisons populated by demotivated inmates.

So what is leadership? One definition suggests that it is a process through which certain people influence the actions, attitudes, and values of others. But who are these 'certain people'? Everyone has, at some time or other, harboured the idea of being a leader. But most people spend the whole of their lives on the receiving end of orders which are to be obeyed, maybe even without question.

Leadership theories

There was an idea circulating in history which suggested that certain people have been born to lead. Earlier historians have investigated the lives of these leaders, and put forward the idea that these people possessed key traits which made them stand out from others. But later research does not confirm these findings. On the contrary, leaders and others are considered not to differ in a clear or concise way in terms of traits.

The next theory to hit the news-stand was the suggestion that leaders emerge from individual situations. One IT function may have fallen into deep trouble with its projects which in turn makes demands for a specific type of leader capable of bringing the strategy back on course. The keywords describing the required person could be 'competitive', 'assertive', and a 'decision-maker'. Another IT function may have been almost entirely destroyed by too much competition, too much assertiveness, together with too much emphasis on quick and decisive actions by the executive in charge. IT specialists may have left in droves and end-users been antagonized, all of which resulted in the IT executive being asked to find another job! The new leader is required to be someone with adequate IT technical skills but, more importantly, to possess exceptional interpersonal skills which will lead to a healing of the broken relationships with end-users in the organization. This leadership approach demands a matching of the skills and qualities of the individual with the situational demands of the organization. It has been criticized because it does not take into account in sufficient detail the requirements of subordinates.

Leaders do not operate in a vacuum. They are influenced by the perceptions, attitudes, and values of their subordinates. This led to the development of an approach called 'transactional' theory. The theory suggests that leadership is a reciprocal flow of influences between leaders and subordinates. It is a synthesis of traits, situations, and the characteristics of subordinates. Leadership is considered to be more about the social nature of relationships.

Are there substitutes for leadership?

Recent research findings suggest that job performance can be directly and indirectly affected by many factors which may ultimately substitute for leadership.[8] Leaders are supposed to exert major influences upon everything around them. But there are leaders who can only be described as figureheads – they have little effect on the human resources or the organization in general. Some would say that this last group should not be called leaders. But the emerging IT environment will include functions which operate more effectively with managers who are not of the traditional leader type. The high technical/commercial knowledge of the leader's subordinates may suggest a figurehead style, or the structure of the jobs make direction and constant supervision redundant. The norms and cohesion of the work groups may not require the presence of a formal leader. During the 1990s fewer full-time middle managers and supervisors will be required because of changes in the organization of work. Teleworking will be scheduled and monitored by corporate computing facilities. This is already happening in some electronic mail applications where each individual's action response time to messages is monitored.

We agree with the comments made by Peter F. Drucker:

> We are entering a period of change, the shift from the command-and-control organization, the organization of departments and divisions, to the information-based organization, the organization of knowledge specialists. We can perceive, though perhaps only dimly, what this organization will look like. We can identify some of its main characteristics and requirements. We can point to central problems of values, structure, and behaviour. But the job of actually building the information-based organization is still ahead of us - it is the management challenge of the future'.[9]

Many hands make light work, but do too many cooks spoil the broth?

Decision-making is a large part of being a manager. Some would go as far as to say decision-making is the essence of managing. We believe there are many connections between decision-making processes in the IT environment, and the optimum utilization and productivity of the human resources.

Many people are happy to carry out actions based on decisions of others – even if the decisions are wrong! Fewer are prepared to take on the responsibility for making decisions, probably because they do not relish the possibility of being wrong and having nobody to blame but themselves.

The process of decision-making

What is a decision-making process? There have been many attempts at defining the most effective procedure, and we will use a basic example:

- The problem must be identified. The elements of the difficulties must be recognized. Identification is not easy, there can be problems recognizing the problem! Perception has a great deal to do with the situation. For example, two people are sitting either side of a table in the company restaurant and looking at a cracked mug which is leaking coffee over the table. They see the problem from two different aspects. The first person sees it as a left-handled mug which is leaking, the second person sees it as right-handled mug which is leaking. The disagreement is about how the mug is perceived. But until one person shifts his or her position of viewing, or alternatively redefines the problem by revolving the mug, they could argue about their perceptions throughout eternity. Meanwhile the mug will continue to leak until all the coffee has spread across the table. Clearly the problem is the leaking crack in the mug and the state of the table, and yet the arguments have been about individual perception of the mug.

- The objectives to be met in solving the problem must be defined. In the example of the cracked mug, the first person sees the objective to be a modification of corporate purchasing policies for mugs. The second person believes the company's maintenance department should change its policies for protecting tables. They may decide the objectives are the development of short-term emergency procedures, coupled with strategic changes to purchasing and maintenance policies. The various solutions will be evaluated in the light of the objective(s).
- A decision has to be taken about how to take the decision. Should the two people sitting at the table sort the problem out for themselves? Should they delegate the decision to others in their work group? Should they call in a consultant who has specialist knowledge of dealing with the problems of cracked mugs leaking coffee? Should they access the computer-based decision support system for advice and guidance? All these queries raise a further question. Do many hands make light work when it comes to making effective decisions?
- The various options for solving the problem have to be identified. The purchasing policies could be modified for mugs – only heavy-duty mugs will be purchased. The maintenance department could coat all existing tables with a substance which will protect them from any future leakages from existing stocks of mugs. Emergency actions could include the immediate disposal of the mug to avoid a repeat of the situation, cleaning the table, and then deciding whether to give all tables a protective coating and/or purchase a different model of mug.
- Each option for solving the problem has to be evaluated. Some may be more effective than others, some may be more difficult to implement.
- A choice has to be made between the various evaluated options.
- The final step is to follow up the results of implementing the chosen option and monitor the effectiveness of the decision. Are there still problems with mugs and tables? Have other problems been caused by implementing the solution?

The message is that decision-making is more than just making choices. Simply making choices in an undisciplined way about human resources in the information technology environment will certainly lead to poor utilization and low productivity.

Decisions in the information technology environment

Some decisions have major strategic implications, others are inconsequential. Managers make decisions about situations where the possible outcomes are well known, and sometimes about problems where the results are more uncertain. The latter is very much the case with human resource problems.

Many highly motivated decision-making managers continually search for a systematic approach to dealing with people problems. Unfortunately, making decisions about human resources is to walk through a minefield – people do not respond on every occasion in a rational way. For example, in a recruitment situation, there could be a requirement for a systems programmer. Several systems programmers are interviewed, and because the the Systems Support Manager is under heavy pressure of work, he decides to select the best candidate seen in the first few days of the recruitment campaign. One view of the Systems Support Manager's behaviour would be that he had not allowed for an optimal decision because he brought the recruitment process to a halt too quickly – there were other candidates in the pipeline. Another view would be that the Systems Support Manager was correct to accept a candidate considered good enough for the appointment on the basis that project pressures demanded a quick recruitment. Although CVs for all the candidates were available, a decision had to be made without detailed interviewing of all the potentially suitable applicants. The Systems Support Manager did not have full information, CVs and interview results for all candidates, so he was in no position to know whether or not he made the best decision.

Some situations allow for optimum decisions, in other words all possible solutions are considered. This is usually the case with most computer hardware and software. Human resource decisions tend too often towards the concept of 'satisficing' – solutions are considered as they become available and the first option which meets the requirement is selected. This approach may be acceptable in the short term where there are manning problems with projects, but it is questionable when considering the medium and longer-term human resource management policies. There is an analogy which compares the two types of decisions: making an optimum decision is like searching a haystack for the sharpest needle, but making a satisficing decision is like searching a haystack for a needle just sharp enough with which to sew.[10]

Work groups and decisions

A corporate IT environment usually has a surfeit of decision-making work groups: committees, various types of study teams, project groups, strategy review boards, etc. All of these groups are charged with the responsibility of making appropriate decisions to ensure optimum return on the company's investment in information technology. But what are the strengths and weaknesses of these decision-making groups? Are group decisions any more likely to succeed than decisions made by an individual?

We believe effective decisions are directly related to the way in which the decision-making is structured. Research suggests that an individual will not perform any better in a structured decision process than a work group.[11] Work groups with correctly structured tasks will make more accurate decisions, although they take longer to reach them. The work groups need to have the necessary knowledge and skills, and be capable of pooling them. We recognize there is the danger of pooling ignorance!

The building of groups, especially those responsible for making decisions about the IT environment and its supporting strategies, is a task requiring much skill. If decisions are required on badly structured tasks, there will be a need for much creativity on the part of the work group members. But creativity is more likely to emerge in a situation where one individual is making decisions and seeing them through. A group structure can all too easily destroy creativity – too many cooks can spoil the broth. Work groups should encourage their members to share knowledge and experience, but they should not be allowed to replace individuals. If this does happen, the utilization and productivity of the human resources will be reduced.

The creativeness of group decision-making can be improved by a number of techniques, the most well-known being 'brainstorming'. But for this method to be effective, the work group members must obey certain basic rules:

* They must avoid criticizing each other's suggestions.
* They must be prepared to offer 'outrageous' thoughts.
* They must attempt to generate as many ideas as possible.
* They must be able to extend other work group members' ideas.

Group decision-making can become caught up in 'groupthink'. Many an IT function over the years has stood accused of being introvert, concentrating on the technology to the exclusion of the commercial requirements expressed by line management. Work groups can isolate themselves from the world outside. Members in very cohesive groups may have more confidence in the group's decisions than any differing ideas of their own. So their critical faculty is switched off and they conform to the work group. This can lead to very dangerous situations when developing major strategies for information technology, especially those aspects which are concerned with the human resources. Group decisions can become totally irrational.

When developing a medium to longer-term plan for information technology, there are times when a project has to be considered which will require the taking of great risks. The risks could include destabilizing existing operational systems and demotivating the human resources. The work group realizes that if the project is implemented successfully, it will deliver major benefits to the company. Will a work group make a riskier or more conservative decision than an individual?

Given the interaction of views, skills, and experience within a work group, you might feel there is more chance of avoiding risky decisions compared with those made by an individual. But systematic research shows that groups tend to make more extreme decisions than individuals.[12] The tendency is for work group members who favour a particular course of action to become more in favour, whilst members who do not support the action become even less in favour. Work groups do not make riskier decisions, the tendency is towards more extreme decisions.

Are there differences between listening and hearing?

A Zen master asked his students a question which has always intrigued us as human resource management and IT specialists: 'If a tree falls in a forest and there is nobody near to hear it fall, is there a noise?'. There is no single answer, but we learn more about ourselves and the environment around us if we allow the question to stir our thoughts. Maybe the question cannot be answered!

However, the question prompts us to think about the actions of listening and hearing. What are their connections with communication as one of the ways to improve utilization and productivity of human resources in the expanding IT environment? There is no guarantee that, once a management decision has been taken about change, written up in a report, circulated to and read by all concerned, it will lead to effective action. People listen to communications, but they do not always hear the message.

Understanding communication

Knowledge, information, and their effective use are the key factors which will lead to the competitive success of commercial organizations in the 1990s. Companies have specialists in information management, technical communications, human resource management, corporate relations, and all the various line management functions, each determined to communicate.

It is suggested by some of the researchers that managers spend eighty per cent of their time speaking, listening, and reading various types of communications. These communications are subject to mis-understanding due to the noise-distortion which is always present when two or more people attempt to communicate with each other. When two people face each other across a table, with or without a cracked mug leaking coffee, the possibilities for misunderstanding are legion.

A project leader praises the work of fellow members in the work group. A new member of the Information Centre reads the advisory manual for helping the end-users to help themselves. A senior computer operator, standing next to a noisy high-speed output printer, attempts to give instructions to junior operational staff about controlling the equip-ment. The IT manager produces a written report which makes recom-mendations for new hardware and software required for the 1990s, and sends it to his CEO to gain top management support.

Each of these situations contains some form of interaction – the human resources are attempting to communicate with each other.

The process of communicating

There are a number of steps associated with human communications:

- A work group or an individual identifies information which has to be communicated to other work groups or another individual.
- The information has to be developed (encoded).
- A medium for transferring the information has to be selected. It may be a written report, a face-to-face discussion, or a sophisticated presentation using audiovisual aids.
- The receiving work group or individual has the task of converting (decoding) the medium to fit into their own ways of dealing with information.
- The receiving work group or individual responds by recognizing the need for agreeing or disagreeing with the information.
- The answer containing the information has to be developed (encoded).
- A decision has to be taken about the medium to be used.
- The original work group then has the task of converting (decoding) the medium to fit into their own ways of dealing with information.

Clearly in all these steps in the communications process there is room for much misunderstanding, much less hearing the message. In the complex area of information technology there are many problems to be overcome when attempting to communicate ideas and strategies.

Why are some people better at communicating than others?

People judged to be good communicators are those who recognize the need to keep all information short and simple. Information must not exceed the capabilities of the receiving work group or individual.

The abilities of human resources to process new information are not infinite. If a work group or individual receives information containing too many ideas expressed in words, numbers, and visual aids, there comes a point when their systems for comprehension break down – the information is lost, never mind the message.

Work groups and individuals have to monitor their capabilities for communicating information. It is too easy not to be sensitive to the amount of information other work groups or individuals can accept. Recognizing overload is an essential quality for all those communicating ideas, especially those associated with change.

Good communicators always recognize the limitations of the medium being used to carry their messages. We ourselves, whilst preparing this publication, have been acutely aware of the limitations of book format as the medium for communicating the complex challenges and opportunities associated with managing people in the information technology environment. There is so much information to be encoded and decoded in the process of understanding the strategic implications of human resource management and information technology. In book format we are not able to monitor the transmission rate, or the level of noise which might develop in the lines of communication between ourselves and readers. We have no way of influencing the approach used by readers to access the information, knowledge and experience expressed in these pages. A reader may enter the process via the contents page, the index, or dip here and there amongst the subjects which seem immediately applicable to the local situations. Our only solution is to structure a logical approach to the topics, pass through a seemingly endless refining process before reaching the final manuscript, and hope that readers are not overloaded with too many ideas so that our essential messages are lost.

Communication is influenced by physical factors

Non-verbal communication can influence the utilization and productivity of human resources. Facial expressions and body movements can have as much impact as the written word. Carefully structured plans can be demolished by the manner and tone of voice used in discussions. We have numerous examples of IT projects which have failed due to the attitudes of project leaders, IT specialists and end-users. The skills were present, the time and finance allocated were adequate, the requirements were specified correctly, and yet the projects failed. Team members' attitudes and behaviour, expressed in body language and the physical state of their offices, lead to a collapse in the relationships between team members, end-users, and their managers. Everyone forgets that human resources do not respond always in a rational manner, and this can be passed on as negative communication through physical factors.

Organizational structure influences the quality of communication

When structuring a work group it is essential to consider the requirements for communication both within the work group and between work groups. To be effective, communications must be able to flow in many directions – the horizontal and vertical needs must be taken into account. Also it has to be recognized that formal and informal communication flows coexist within all organization structures.

An IT function consists of many sub-units, and there will be formal lines of communication between the sub-units. Certain sub-units will have close relationships with end-users, and in turn these will be supported by more formal communications. All these communication links build up into major networks which sustain the life of the organization.

Performance is linked to the quality and shape of these networks. There are a variety of network types, but most can be classified as either centralized or decentralized. The centralized networks are dependent upon one point through which all communications must flow, whilst the decentralized alternatives are based on many people interacting, there being no single control point. Simple tasks can be supported by a centralized network; more complex tasks (involving many more people) require decentralized procedures. Implementing the wrong form of communications procedure for a work group and the surrounding organization will lead to poor utilization of human resources and low levels of productivity.

Never forget the power of informal communication

Every organization possesses an informal communication network – the grapevine. It is powerful and should not be overlooked. Like the formal communications network, a grapevine can work to support the objectives of the organization or it can destroy management's best endeavours.

Research findings suggest that eighty per cent of the information carried in corporate grapevines is correct.[13] But like all 80/20 rules, attention should be drawn to the twenty per cent. These are the communications which may well cause serious trouble – most human resource management specialists will confirm that incorrect rumours of reorganization and redundancy frequently float around in the grapevines.

Given the existence of the grapevines, positive information has to be put into them throughout the development and implementation of strategies for human resource management and information technology.

Has information technology provided tools to improve the utilization and productivity of the human resources?

We would answer the question with a qualified yes. Whilst writing this book, we have witnessed the introduction of fairly sophisticated software tools, all of which purport to be concerned with saving labour in the development areas of the information technology environment. In a period of just under two years, the range of products has risen from a small number to at least several hundred tools – their utility and quality varying considerably. There is a discrepancy between the marketing claims for the software and the comments we have been given by IT managers and specialists using the tools. The term 'productivity improvement' has become fashionable in the information technology sphere. Many of these products have been rushed on to the market, and there have been exaggerated claims made about their performance. The specialists using the tools have mixed views about their effectiveness.

What is a productivity improvement software tool?

Information technology functions are constantly struggling with the major problems of maintaining existing applications and attempting to support the huge backlog of demands from end-users. Earlier programming languages such as COBOL and BASIC are powerful, but they require programmers to produce a great deal of coding. There have been attempts to increase the productivity of programmers by using structured programming methodologies. However, the traditional application development process is lengthy and inflexible – defining the user requirements, producing specifications, prototyping, coding, and updating with subsequent amendments requested by end-users.

More advanced programming methods – 4th Generation Languages (4GLs) – have been introduced to overcome these problems. A 4GL should give a programmer a more powerful way of developing applications because the language is supposed to take less time to learn, needs less coding and less documentation, and less maintenance – hence improved productivity.

Are there differences of approach amongst the 4GLs?

There are two types of software packages marketed as 4GLs:

- There are products which are considered to be functional replace-ments for the earlier programming languages. These types of 4GLs help IT technical specialists to overcome the maintenance problems associated with monolithic application programs operating in a centralized data processing environment. Examples of products in this group are NATURAL, IDEAL, PRO-IV, and Powerhouse.
- The second group are software products designed to support end-users and IT specialist personnel working in Information Centres to help end-users help themselves. These packages include enhanced versions of earlier software which allow the relatively quick genera-tion of reports and the processing of queries against master files of information. Examples of products in the second group are Focus, SAS, Ramis II and Nomad II.

The 4GLs are supposed to be easier to use and more powerful than the earlier programming languages. Accessing data in computer files is simpler because programmers do not have to instruct the machine how to fetch the data – programmers just specify the data they require.

Success and failure

In some instances 4GLs have produced significant gains in productivity, and they are supported enthusiastically by their users. However, we found several technical users who were not too happy with the results achieved. Success and failure were connected with the way a tool was being used, rather than the quality of the software. To use a sophisticated hand drill to hammer in a nail indicates some level of misunderstanding on the part of the technical user! There were examples of application development personnel holding 'luddite' attitudes towards these new tools.

4GLs may be easier to use than the earlier programming languages, more cost-effective and powerful, but they are not so articulate. Gains are made in productivity, but there is a loss in flexibility.

Whilst COBOL is standardized and supplied by a number of vendors, 4GLs suffer from too many variations on the basic theme – there are major fundamental differences between individual packages. Choosing a 4GL means assessing a number of trade-offs. For example, to make a gain in productivity may require a sacrifice in processing speeds.

Many programmers and end-users utilizing 4GLs admit they are not simple to use. A 4GL is sold as a 'tool kit', but it can take an experienced programmer four or five months to become proficient. Most organiza-tions cannot contemplate technical specialists being unproductive for such a lengthy period.

Providing the less experienced end-users with more powerful tools presents a range of problems. It is not too difficult for unsuspecting end-users to find themselves running into major problems accessing a database. One example is quoted by Codd:

> A database residing in the USA and the UK is linked by telephone. The end-user in the USA wants to know the supplier numbers of London-based suppliers of red parts. IBM's SQL is used to make the query and the list is available in just over one second. In the worst case, though, the list takes more than two days to complete.

Although more and more companies are considering the implementation of 4GLs, most maintenance undertaken by programmers is not due to poor programming, but is rooted in the inadequate analysis and design of the original application. Mistakes in programming can be rectified relatively easily and quickly. It is bad design of applications which leads to constant and lengthy maintenance difficulties.

The 4GLs will have to co-exist with programs developed via the earlier programming languages. This means that 4GLs will have to be able to call in program modules written in other languages such as COBOL and BASIC. Currently, there is little chance of integrating existing code with 4GL applications. IT specialists do not have the time to rewrite all the existing programs in 4GLs, so they are concentrating on using them in new applications.

We believe the mix of old and new applications using earlier programming languages and 4GLs will provide many challenges for technical managers and end-users looking for major productivity improvements, much less improved utilization of the human resources.

What is the connection between 4GLs and CASE?

Whilst investigating the implementation and performance of certain 4GLs, we discovered some were disappearing into a new generalized concept known as Computer Assisted Systems Engineering (CASE). CASE includes a wide range of packages associated with developing and supporting program development. All the packages have the objective of encouraging closer end-user/IT specialist co-operation in the application development process. This should reduce the maintenance burden on IT personnel, allow for improved utilization and higher productivity of the specialists, and ensure end-users influence the development of systems.

Advantages and disadvantages of the CASE approach

One example of CASE leading to improved productivity is the DuPont organization in the USA. The company used Cortex's Application Factory and Corvision CASE products on fifteen system development projects. DuPont estimates it has made savings of over $2.3 million. The applications varied enormously, but each CASE project had at least three things in common:

- All applications were completed on time and within budget.
- All were completed in less time than it would have taken to write out a formal specification for a COBOL program.
- All were completed at a lower cost than modifying an off-the-shelf application package.

The IT development manager of another company states that CASE tools perform better in some areas than others. The tools make dramatic improvements in productivity when developing screen-based systems and fairly simple reports. But the improvements were not as great for complex reports and search systems.

If the CASE tools are to be exploited fully, it is important for them to be used in an environment which includes a sophisticated development methodology. There has to be a firm specification of a system before attempting to use CASE tools for building it. The CASE tools are the way of automating the development methodology.

CASE and the human resources

CASE has several major implications for human resource management policies and strategies.

Moving into a CASE environment requires a high level of training in the tools and the supporting development methodologies. Several companies have made the mistake of attempting to use CASE without a development methodology. This has led to problems during the training of specialists and end-users – they lacked understanding or experience of a structured development methodology which made it difficult for them to see CASE in context during their courses.

The key work elements of analysis and design will diminish. A number of CASE tools can now automatically generate a physical database schema direct from high-level entity diagrams. This will allow the systems analysts to concentrate more on the business aspects of the development process. But not all systems analysts are business-literate, and their future recruitment and training will need to concentrate more on business issues. One methodology specialist said:

> Traditionally, business training has been considered an unnecessary extravagance for IT personnel. Effort has gone into producing technical experts. Wrongly, many companies try to train IT personnel from the bottom up – first as programmers, then turn them into designers, then into analysts, and finally into business analysts. The approach simply produces IT professionals whose technical basis precludes them from understanding business, and the result is that they produce systems that simply do not match business requirements.

CASE will influence the traditional programming function. Already program code generating tools such as IEF, APS, Gamma and Quickbuild are having an impact. Other products, such as Automate, Excelerator,

IEW and Page, are automating the analysis and design activities.

Although certain technical units such as performance management and systems programming will survive, many of the applications development activities will be carried out with highly automated, code-generating CASE tools.

IT personnel are beginning to be trained from the top down, beginning with the business issues, then progressing to how development methodologies and CASE can assist them to build effective business systems. There will be a positive impact on the attitudes of IT personnel. Currently, they tend towards having a close affinity with the job being performed, rather than for their organization. This means they are highly mobile, moving from one company to another in quick succession. Business training will provide IT staff with an affinity for the organization, and we believe high levels of labour turnover will be reduced.

Better utilization and higher productivity of the human resources demands an integrated approach

We have emphasized the need to be aware of many different factors which influence the utilization and productivity of human resources in the IT environment:

- The links between job satisfaction and performance.
- The elements which make performance appraisal a positive activity.
- The complexity of work groups and their interaction.
- The qualities which make for effective leadership.
- The importance of structuring decision-making to ensure improved quality of decisions.
- The problems encountered when communicating ideas and strategies.
- The part to be played by information technology itself via 4GLs and CASE productivity improvement tools.

Implementing a range of activities and policies leading to the required improvements demands an approach which is comprehensive and practical. Concentration on any one single factor is not likely to result in the improvements sought. We believe tinkering about here and there with activities and policies will be a waste of time. Careful audit and review are essential before attempting to develop a remedial programme. We include suggestions for structuring an approach to such an audit amongst the appendices to this book.

The comprehensive approach to human resource management for the IT environment, which we discuss in Chapter 8, requires inputs from all the areas influencing the utilization and productivity of human resources.

Notes and references

1   E. A. Locke, 'The nature and causes of job satisfaction' in *Handbook of Industrial and Organizational Psychology*, ed. M. Dunnette (Rand McNally, 1976).
2   L. W. Porter and E. E. Lawler, *Managerial Attitudes and Performance* (Dorsey Press, 1968).
3   T. S. Bateman and D. W. Organ, 'Job satisfaction and the good soldier: the relationship between affect and employee citizenship', *Academy of Management Journal*, **26**, pp. 587-595, 1983.
4   P. Long, *Performance Appraisal Revisited* (Institute of Personnel Management, 1986).
5   Tom Philp, *Making Performance Appraisal Work* (McGraw-Hill, 1983).
6   I. L. Janis, *Groupthink: Psychological Studies of Policy Decisions and Fiascos* (Houghton Mifflin, 1982).
7   I. D. Steiner, 'Task performing groups', an article in *Contemporary Topics in Social Psychology* (General Learning, 1976).
8   J. E. Sheridan, D. J. Vredenburgh and M. A. Abelson, 'Contextual model of leadership influence in hospital units', *Academy of Management Journal*, **27**, pp. 57-58, 1984.
9   Peter F. Drucker, 'The coming of the new organization', *Harvard Business Review*, Jan-Feb 1988.
10 J. G. March and H. A. Simon, *Organizations* (John Wiley, 1958).
11 R. A. Weber, 'The relationship of group performance to the age of members in homogeneous groups', *Academy of Management Journal*, **17**, pp. 570-574, 1974.
12 H. Lamm and D. G. Myers, 'Group-induced polarization of attitudes and behaviour', ed. L. Berkowitz, *Advances in Experimental Social Psychology*, vol 11 (Academic Press, 1978).
13 E. Walton, 'How efficient is the grapevine?', *Personnel*, **28**, pp. 45-49, 1961.

CHAPTER 8

MANPOWER PLANNING AND THE IT ENVIRONMENT

The most carefully conceived business objectives and corporate plans will fail if there are insufficient people with the right skills and abilities to carry them out at the appropriate time. This is very much the case in the area of Information Technology.

In the past comparatively little has been done to ensure that IT manpower as well as marketing, production and finance is taken into account when future corporate developments are discussed. There have been occasions when an important commercial project has had to be abandoned, relocated or adapted significantly because IT labour requirements cannot be met. Remedying shortages of other resources at short notice may be costly and embarrassing. Remedying an IT labour shortage, using contract staff or external facilities, can be no less expensive and may at times be completely impossible within the timescale laid down.

Emphasis on IT manpower planning in recent years has come from recognition of the fact that informed anticipation of future needs and plans to meet any shortfalls or surpluses will help to avoid emergency action and lay a more stable foundation for the years ahead. Sophisticated techniques are now available to predict the numbers and skills that will be called for and those likely to be available. While forecasting can never be an exact science, the use of computer and other models to test various assumptions and to establish trends has proved a refinement that has added to its accuracy, and the element of guesswork has been substantially reduced.

The objective of effective manpower planning for the information technology environment is to maintain the appropriate critical mass of technical and commercial knowledge, albeit in new roles, and the fore-casting of new skill requirements. More companies should be implementing this aspect of HRM.

Background

Manpower planning can be defined as: *a method of trying to establish an organization's manpower requirements in terms of quantity and quality for a specified period of time, and determining how these requirements might be met.* A number of additional points need to be borne in mind.

Planning is about reducing future uncertainties – this is equally important for an organization and for its employees. Unforeseen IT employee surpluses or shortages can both badly affect an organization's competitiveness, and be very difficult to rectify. Similarly the future of employees should not be a matter of random guesswork, or decided suddenly in reaction to some crisis. Few major changes in a company's IT operations take place overnight and cannot to some extent be anticipated, even in a volatile environment. It is mutually advantageous to anticipate changes and effect them as gradually and as painlessly as possible on the basis of more long-term if less spectacular plans. If there is some agreed procedure for examining closely the manpower implications at an early stage, both the company and its employees reap the benefit from the longer period they will have to prepare for change.

Is it, however, possible to plan an organization's IT human resources – managers, specialists and end-users – in the same way as its capital resources or raw materials? People are not passive objects to be manipu-lated but subject to the vagaries of individual behaviour. Manpower planning encourages the development of a better understanding of how people behave in an organizational setting, a worthwhile exercise in itself from an employee relations point of view. Any individual's behaviour may not be predictable but behavioural trends can be predicted with a high degree of accuracy, given sufficient information and careful analysis. Even if forecasts are not entirely reliable, the collection of infor-mation needed to make them often brings to light potential troublespots.

Manpower planning is not purely a question of matching manpower supply and manpower demand. In planning what may well be an organization's most expensive resource, especially in labour-intensive industries, productivity considerations and the most efficient use of manpower should be part of any manpower plan, especially for infor-mation technology. Manpower 'demand' has increasingly to be justified on a cost basis and subject to financial controls. The ability of a firm to compete may well depend on how closely future labour costs are pre-dicted and controlled.

Manpower planning in the past has often failed because it has become too much the domain of the statistician and the economist and divorced from business plans. It is not a statistical exercise conducted without reference to the objectives of the organization but an integral part of corporate strategy. If a company is examining and determining its strategic objectives for a period of five years ahead, it can scarcely ignore the IT manpower implications of these objectives.

The development of a 'Manpower Plan' is not a once and for all activity, but part of a dynamic process which is constantly under review and constantly being modified – a process in which forecasts are checked against reality and models and assumptions are constantly evaluated.

These points will be borne in mind when looking at the history and operation of manpower planning in the high technology company already discussed in Chapter 5. We have divided our review into three main stages:

- *Demand forecasting*, estimating future IT manpower needs by reference to business plans and forecasts of future levels of activity.
- *Supply forecasting*, estimating the supply of manpower from inside and outside the organization by analysing current resources and future availability, after allowing for wastage.
- *Action plans*, necessary to deal with any future deficits or surpluses.

Before manpower planning was introduced into the company as a whole, very little thought was given to the number of people that could be supported by the company, indeed it was difficult to gain agreement on how many people the company actually employed!

A start was made during the 1970s to develop manpower planning for one site of the company. The Manpower Planning Manager agitated for the approach to be used throughout the company. He foresaw the effects of technology and IT development on manpower.

At the beginning of the 1980s, due to commercial pressures on the company, manpower planning became a critical issue due to changes in the market, collapse of orders, poor company planning and decision-making, and costs rising too fast. In particular, over seventy per cent of sales revenue went in labour costs. From the outset the company's manpower planning was based on improved performance objectives. The first Company Plan was introduced on that basis and integrated with business planning. It has never been solely a question of balancing supply with demand. Since manpower planning has been in operation the company has achieved a planned reduction in total staff of thirty-six per cent and labour costs have been reduced to below forty per cent of sales revenue.

Forecasting manpower demand

Manpower requirements are arrived at by a joint process of 'top-down' modelling and 'bottom-up' plans and forecasts. On the one hand, manpower forecasts are derived from the corporate business plan and are circulated downwards for discussion; on the other hand, line managers are asked to estimate future needs and pass these estimates up through the hierarchy for collation and comment.

The 'top-down' modelling aspect

The company's manpower plan starts off on a theoretical basis. Corporate Planning, with computer assistance, works out predictions of future company performance targets in areas such as orders, manufacturing, development, and profitability. Techniques used would vary from simple extrapolation (predicting the growth and decline of a single variable), through regression analysis (to establish the extent to which movements in the value of two or more variables are related), to complex econometric modelling (where an attempt would be made to establish a relationship between a number of variables affecting the business). This would give a picture of the business plans for the company, possibly taking a best, worst and middle view of the corporate future. An integral part of this picture would be a manpower projection. An initial calculation of manpower in this way has the advantage of not necessarily being constrained by past practices, which may need to change fairly radically in the future, particularly in a high technology industry.

The business plan indicates, on the basis of business assumptions, the performance targets and revenues. These are proactive in the sense that the company wants to achieve them. Costs are also predicted, including manpower costs. Given that the inflation scenario envisaged proves to be correct, manpower costs may be predicted to an accuracy of 0.3 per cent per year. This is worked out on the basis of predicted average pay cost per head – taking into account how basic salary costs, insurance contributions, pensions and overtime, etc., will rise in future years. The same calculations can also be used for working out the cost of a suggested principal annual salary increase of x per cent put up by the trade unions. A labour costs increase of this amount can be simulated to see what the effect would be on the company's profitability. Bearing in mind the constraint that labour costs must not exceed forty per cent of revenue, in any given year the average number of people the Company can afford to employ can be calculated from projected revenue. Put very simply:

$$\frac{\text{revenue for year } n}{\text{average cost per head at year } n} \times \frac{40}{100} = \text{average no. the company can afford to employ}$$

Thus the manpower plan is closely connected with budgets and costs.

An estimate of critical manpower categories could also be made at the company level, e.g. salesmen:

$$\frac{\text{projected revenue for year } n}{\text{individual sales targets}} = \text{number of salesmen required}$$

The number of regions would indicate number of sales managers required.

The business plan for each of the divisions of the company gives an indication of the revenue to be generated by those divisions and therefore an indication of the total manpower allocation and total manpower cost that each function will be able to support.

To summarize, the company plan looks at what the organization can afford to spend on manpower if profit and market targets are to be met. Management has to plan for a workforce – including the IT component – capable of achieving the work to be done within this cost constraint.

The 'bottom-up' aspect

If you cannot remember the structure of the division described in Chapter 5, we will refresh your memory. Each sub-unit consists of 120 people developing a particular high technology product. The sub-units are divided into segments containing approximately fifty people which are further divided into sectors consisting of up to twenty-five people.

The 'bottom-up' aspect is the other side of the planning process, going on in parallel with the company modelling. This process starts from the smallest work group, where a forecast of requirements is produced for the next year ahead, and a breakdown of the forecast into the main IT manpower categories required for achieving the business targets of the sub-unit.

The full-time employee forecast at the end of the current planning year has more or less to tie in with the consolidated company figure. The forecasts are made by the sub-units looking at the work schedules, estimating that they will need 'x' programmers, 'y' engineers, and 'z' team leaders. They would fill in the current total, a forecast of outflows and the inflows anticipated as necessary to compensate for outflows, to give the demand forecast figure for the sub-unit. They would then break their forecast figure down by the most significant manpower categories, showing anticipated outflows to meet their demand for a particular manpower category – the information being extracted from their own records.

The divisional forecast is produced by the Manpower Planning Manager using the sector/segment/sub-unit forecasts. Consultation and negotiation take place at each level regarding numbers and skill profiles.

Each sub-unit manager negotiates at divisional level for his or her share of the manpower allocation, while divisional executives negotiate at company level for their share of the company allocation against other divisions. Finally the sub-unit figures are agreed and consolidated into a divisional picture and the divisional pictures are merged into the company picture.

There is always a certain amount of conflict generated during the 'top-down' modelling and the 'bottom-up' process as sub-units within the division have to compete with each other for limited resources, and as the proposed figures are scrutinized and challenged at each level.

Degree of tolerance

The final agreement between the company and the divisions allows for a small amount of tolerance, for example a freelance specialist or temporary employee might have to be brought in to assist with a project at a particular point. There are also constraints on these areas, which could otherwise undermine the control of costs.

Once the manpower allocation and manpower costs are finalized throughout the company, these have to be adhered to strictly, unless for example planned revenues are exceeded, when extra staff could be eased in. On the whole, however, performance targets must be adhered to. If the trade unions force up manpower costs beyond allocated levels, this will automatically result in job losses.

Productivity considerations

Productivity considerations operate at all levels of the process of determining manpower requirements and settling the manpower allocation.

At company level, productivity ratios are set in areas where there is a significant correlation for the company between different variables and productivity. Some of the ratios used are:

- Revenue: costs.
- Profit: investment.
- Costs: people.
- Pay costs: people.
- Development costs: designers.
- Revenue: people.
- Revenue: salesmen.
- Revenue: service people.
- Investments: people.

The results have to conform to a desired productivity ratio.

Other ratios used are:

- Managers: salesmen.
- Managers: other groups.
- Total numbers: administrative people.
- Directs: indirects.

If, for example, revenue per head increases in relation to pay cost per head, the company can afford to pay people more, otherwise not. Current ratios are always reviewed to see whether they should be improved. These ratios could also be related to the Business Plan for individual divisions to see if the division concerned is conforming to company productivity ratios.

Productivity considerations also operate in divisional and sub-unit bottom-up approaches. The tendency is to overestimate the numbers required if such considerations are not applied to the process. Managers under pressure to meet deadlines may try to incorporate one or two extra staff to allow for this, and may inflate demand in anticipation of cuts that they feel may be made by a higher level.

On what productivity grounds are managerial plans and forecasts judged to be reasonable in the company?

The main factor in keeping down excessive IT manpower demand is the knowledge that every estimate has to be justified to senior levels of management who themselves will be severely penalized for allowing unwarranted manpower growth. For example, any suggested recruitment has to be authorized at senior management level, and this also applies to replacements. As managers are still responsible for meeting their schedules and targets the effect of this constraint is to make them look at ways of improving productivity in their area.

The company does not conduct any work study exercises to look at ways of improving productivity, but inter-site comparisons could be taken into account by senior management. For example, one division has a personnel department of eight, whereas the division under discussion has eighteen people. It may be that the first division is undermanned in this area, but it is not likely that the second division would be permitted to increase its numbers and it might well have to accept cuts, leavers not being replaced, etc.

Managers are required to take account of any technological changes – for example CASE tools – which could improve productivity. Technological advances have had more impact on the manufacturing processes and the products themselves than on the working of the division. One change has affected the manning of computer rooms – the increasing sophistication of computer operating systems is helping to bring about the 'operatorless' computer systems; technology change has reduced manpower demand in this area of the division.

Thus the effect of top-down modelling is to provide a useful yardstick against which to measure bottom-up forecasting, the tension between the two working towards better utilization and productivity of the human resources.

Forecasting manpower supply

Forecasts of future IT labour demand will be of little value unless they are related to the current and future supply position. The manpower planner should have as complete and accurate a picture as possible of the company's existing IT manpower stock. He should be able to estimate in what areas and to what degree this stock will change by the end of the forecasting period.

The obvious way of meeting IT manpower requirements is from people currently employed. The company operates an internal recruitment policy wherever posible. The problem is, however, that the manpower stock is never static and is constantly subject to outflow and inflows (see Figure 8.1).

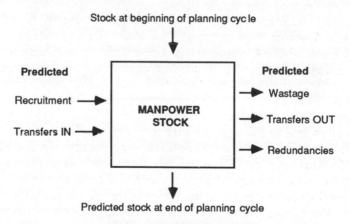

Figure 8.1 Manpower flows

Given an accurate record of current IT manpower stock the most important element in forecasting internal supply is how many people will leave, particularly by voluntary wastage. Certain movements in and out can be known in advance and to some extent controlled by the company, but voluntary wastage has to be predicted. The company can decide how many to promote as it sets the criteria for promotion; it can decide how many to recruit; it will be aware of impending retirements – it cannot control them but it does set the retirement rules and it can modify them (early retirement, etc.). Even the death rate can be predicted accurate to 0.2 per cent using actuarial information! The company cannot determine voluntary wastage other than by predicting it with a high degree of accuracy. Depending on where it is happening it could be regarded as too high or too low – too high if it is in an area of scarce IT skills, too low if it is causing promotional blockages or preventing any new blood coming into the area. Wastage is not something over which the organization has immediate control but accurately predicted it can be an important factor in achieving the manpower levels required by the company.

Natural wastage covers all voluntary and involuntary leaving, apart from redundancies – deaths, retirements, early retirements due to ill health, pregnancy, move to another job, etc.

Crude labour turnover is calculated at corporate level, while survival is calculated at divisional level. If wastage rates are higher than normal, a particular problem area would be identified and an attempt probably made to reduce wastage when it had been analysed in terms of important factors such as length of service, age, sex, occupation, first job effect, losses after training, external environmental opportunities. For example, a few years ago there was a high waste rate on salesmen in the division. Each operating unit was asked to investigate and it was apparent that losses were occurring in the lower age range with one or two years service, i.e. salesmen were coming and going within a short time of joining the company. The exact problem was identified, the salary structure was adjusted and more training and development were provided.

If wastage can be accurately forecast, any obvious abnormalities being smoothed out, the company should have a good idea of the extent to which demand can be met from internal supply. The wastage rate tends to be stable in the organization and easily predictable from past trends. If wastage rates are changing rapidly the Institute of Manpower Studies 'WASP' (Wastage Analysis Statistical Package) could be useful. One of the aims of an organization could be to use predicted levels of total wastage to quantify manpower decisions. Contracting areas in particular should be making extensive use of the data on wastage, as there are legal constraints on dismissing people and it is costly to make them redundant. It is interesting to note that the company used wastage to achieve the thirty-six per cent reduction in staff during the early 1980s. This involved major redundancies in particular areas but was also followed by the use of natural wastage across the board. The problem with allowing natural wastage to run down staff numbers is that inevitably some very skilled staff are lost whom the company would prefer to have retained.

We now need to look at action plans that are generated either if forecast demand looks like exceeding forecast supply or if forecast supply looks like exceeding forecast demand.

Action plans

Forecasting is concerned with demand (the requirement for IT manpower), and supply (the provision of IT manpower). Once a consensus has been reached on the requirement and supply position, action plans can be decided.

Planning and control are concerned with turning forecasts into human resource management policies either to increase, develop, maintain, or decrease the current manpower stock. From the manpower forecasts the company has to decide what changes, if any, are necessary; how they can best be carried out and which particular individuals will be affected. Difficulties can occur when attempting to gain acceptance for perhaps unpopular changes at an individual level. In these areas the HRM function can be of assistance with advice and counselling for those involved in the changes, both managers and their staff.

If IT manpower shortages are forecast, decisions have to be made about recruitment, training, promoting, transferring in, bringing in temporary or freelance staff. If manpower surpluses are forecast, decisions have to be made about stopping recruitment, using natural wastage, early retirements, transfers out, retraining, voluntary redundancies, and compulsory redundancies.

Action plans as a result of the agreed manpower plan are developed by the company at local level, moving from 'What is to be done?' to 'How is it going to be done?'. The whole point of the manpower planning forecasts is that the company is given time to develop appropriate action plans, because shortages or surpluses have been foreseen.

What would happen if an increase in IT manpower were required, assuming that an increase had been justified on productivity grounds and approved at senior management level?

The vacancy would be advertised internally – giving a chance for employee development by means of a transfer in. Or an individual might be groomed for the vacancy by training/reprofiling – he or she might be 'pushed' into it. Individual managers would know their staff, what training they have had, who they could recommend for training. They may have possible succession plans for various key jobs, they know the IT skills range of their people, whether they could be reprofiled. The company could decide to transfer people in from another area that might be running down, giving people career development opportunities. External recruitment might be brought in as a last resort if no suitable candidates were forthcoming from within or if the company wanted to buy in specialist expertise.

The company would have to decide on a policy if there was an IT skills shortage which could not be met in the short term either from internal or external sources. Information Centre staff, for example, have been identified as a key manpower category for the division, but there has been much difficulty obtaining people with the appropriate mix of technical and interpersonal skills. The Manpower Planning Manager has identified the problem and a compaign for obtaining staff is being developed, one suggestion being that the brightest of the graduate intake should be earmarked as Information Centre material. The corporate personnel database might also be actively searched for suitable candidates who could then be approached.

What would happen if decreases of IT manpower were required? (Yes, it can happen!) Certain decisions would have to be made. The total numbers, the sub-units concerned and the manpower categories affected would be shown up in the comparison of the supply and demand forecast in the IT manpower plan. Decisions would have to be made on how to effect the changes. Consultation would take place at corporate level with representatives of all members of the IT workforce, with appropriate local representatives present.

Can the company afford to reduce by means of natural wastage? This depends on the amount of natural wastage forecast in the areas and IT manpower categories concerned, how long it will take and whether the company can afford to wait for natural wastage to take effect.

The company has a security of employment agreement with various trade unions in which it agrees to take measures to try and avoid redundancies. Providing the measures are applicable to the situation, the company agrees to consider discontinuing temporary or contract labour, withdrawing outside contracts, suspending overtime, suspending advertising and recruitment, retirement of personnel on extension of service, short-term work sharing or part-time working. Should redundancies be unavoidable the company would discuss with the trade unions the phasing of the redundancies, the categories of employees involved including any volunteers, and representations on behalf of individuals to be affected. Selection for redundancy would be based on the continuing efficiency of the sub-units, but length of continuous service in the company would be a major consideration, the principle 'last in/first out' being applied.

If redundancy appears to be inevitable another decision to be made is how much notice to give. The company agrees to allow a ninety-day consultative period regardless of the number of employees involved. Over and above this, decisions on how much notice to give have to be based on business considerations and the nature of the redundancies. Some members of a sub-unit operating in the USA know that they will be made redundant when their current project comes to an end. They have known this for a long time and they accept it. On the other hand, it is very difficult to give long notice of running down an IT function where a considerable number of jobs have to go. Projects have to be completed and too much advance warning might result in morale problems and labour troubles. In this case the company would do all it could to help place employees elsewhere immediately the redundancy was announced.

What would happen if IT manpower needs to be transferred from one area to another? This happens from time to time in the division with its sub-units being organized on the project approach. There may be two sub-units each with fifty people working on Project A and Project B respectively. Project A is due to come to an end at the end of the year, whereas Project B will be expanding. The forward review of the manpower plan for the second month of the following year will show that the bulk of the Project A team must be merged with the Project B team by the end of the current year. The fact that this merger has been foreseen and planned does not makes its implementation easy. Local managers have difficult decisions to make about the future of particular individuals and the changes are not achieved without some casualties, even though transfer does not involve loss in salary or loss of status. Labour turnover tends to increase and people are not always satisfied with their particular move. The human resource management team associated with the sub-units would have an important part to play in assisting with this organizational development.

What effect does the operation of manpower planning have on IT career development opportunities? With the total labour force being reduced, thought has to be given to ways in which opportunities can be given to career aspirations. Job vacancies are reduced and with this the chance of promotion into another job. The number of managers is reducing proportionately so upward mobility is constrained throughout the company. When the division stopped recruitment of computer operators, in accordance with the manpower forecast several years ago, and moved towards 'operatorless' systems, recruitment of shift leaders and operations managers was also stopped. The company has to promote people upwards through the grades for the time being rather than into other jobs. As there are fewer people to achieve given targets, jobs are expanding in terms of the amount of work to be done and more variety in the job.

What happens when the IT manpower plan indicates that a different skills balance is required? Re-profiling or retraining is not too much of a problem in the division because the main skills of the largely graduate engineers and programmers are their ability to learn and adapt in a development environment. For electronics engineers the main changes have been miniaturization and cheaper production. Programmers learn programming languages relatively quickly and they adapt to the more gradual software systems changes over the years.

Running and monitoring the manpower planning system

Manpower planning operations are supported at corporate level and are regarded as an integral part of corporate planning and of business planning strategies at all levels. The utilization and productivity of the company's human resources is a key factor in the company's profitability. Manpower figures throughout the company have become visible and top management can quickly see what is happening on this front. The primary prerequisite for obtaining these figures is a comprehensive and up-to-date record of personnel data for every employee. Where a company has a standardized system of personnel records covering all its departments and divisions, much of the information needed will be readily available, particularly if the information is already held on a computer.

The company's personnel file

The computerized personnel record system was extended in the early 1980s for manpower planning purposes. This file is not combined with the payroll file but it is easy to transfer information from one file to the other. The corporate personnel file is held on a mainframe computer at one of the company's data centres, whilst the division has a local personnel record system operating on its own computing facilities which is in turn linked to the mainframe.

The personnel record

The personnel record is very large and contains extensive historical data. The following types of information are held:

- Personnel details (name, initials and title, unique personal number, sex, date of birth, date of joining/source of recruitment, date of leaving, reasons for leaving).
- Location in company (organization code, location code for division and sub-unit).
- Job code (the company has over 600 job codes). It is a powerful coding system showing direct, indirect and general grouping as well as skills.
- Manpower categories (there are 100 categories).
- Job knowledge and education (job knowledge, promotion rating, education, qualifications, training, foreign languages). This enables the company to draw on a supply of people with knowledge and skills appropriate to a given job.
- Costs (salary history, grade, other payments such as overtime, etc.). Manpower cannot be related to business needs nor can effective

manpower strategies be developed without bringing in cost. People cost money – decisions to change the composition of the IT workforce will have their financial consequences. As a basis for estimating these, an individual's salary level and job-related payments must be included.

- Historical details (the history of a person's career with the company). All the jobs held since joining the organization can give a complete picture of the nature of the workforce at any given time.

File updating process

As important as the type and amount of detailed information held are the procedures set up to maintain an up-to-date and accurate personnel record system. In the division two human resource management specialists are responsible for salaries, personnel records and statistics, and an administrator is responsible for the daily updating of the divisional personnel file. Obtaining change information from the sub-units is not a problem.

Running the system

Company planning extends over a five-year period, and manpower planning (with the IT component) is integrated with it, a five-year look at manpower being taken on a top-down, bottom-up, basis. From this overall plan an annual plan is drawn up in more detail prior to each financial year covered by the plan. To date the overall plan has not been subject to major revisions, and each year has seen the appropriate part of the plan carried out with only minor variations.

Stages in the planning process

The corporate financial year runs from January to December. The planning process for the 1990 annual planning process, for example, will start in June 1989. As a result of the annual top-down and bottom-up processes, a draft plan would be arrived at for the year ahead. This would show the current manpower stock by sub-unit and by significant manpower category, the forecast 'ins' and 'outs' for the year, and the manpower forecast for the end of the year.

Monthly reports

A close check between the forecasts and what has actually happened is carried out by means of monthly reports. These reports are produced by the human resource management team on behalf of the sub-units. They show all changes that have occurred during the past month with comments on any trends. Copies are sent to Finance, the sub-unit managers and the Divisional Director to see whether there is any need to adjust the plan.

Quarterly reviews

These are carried out by the manager of each organizational unit and contain the last quarter's actual information. On the basis of the forecasts and the last quarter's actual information a review takes place conducted by the Divisional Director, who looks at all the business ratios, man-power allocation, etc., in the light of what has happened.

Summary of use and effectiveness of manpower planning

Uses of manpower planning in the company

Manpower planning has provided accurate information about the company's future manpower demand and supply position, thus enabling manpower decisions, including those for the IT environment, to be made as a result of informed choices. Senior management have been able to take manpower decisions with more confidence because they always have available an accurate and up-to-date picture of the company's manpower situation. Manpower planning has promoted better manpower utilization and productivity throughout the company as manpower numbers and costs have to be justified in relation to the business revenue generated.

The manpower costing exercises associated with the manpower demand forecasts put the company in a stronger negotiating position with the trade unions. The company can predict what the cost of any given pay settlement will be and is able to say whether the company can afford it.

By predicting future surpluses or shortages, the company is given time to decide the best course of action. Predicted shortages of key staff can be identified and campaigns undertaken to recruit, train or develop staff in these areas. Manpower planning helps to predict organizational changes by linking business growth or cutbacks to particular corporate units.

The system of manpower planning, with the bottom-up aspect and reliance on managers to decide exactly how plans are to be implemented in their areas, allows considerable scope for individual managerial judgment, within overall business constraints.

Effectiveness of manpower planning in the company

The main area of effectiveness has been the accuracy of the predictions coming out of the manpower planning process. The supply forecast is accurate to plus or minus one per cent over a three-year period. Pay costs are accurately predicted to plus or minus 0.3 per cent annually (even taking into account variations in the inflation scenario). Shortages in key areas and manpower categories, such as IT, are accurately predicted because numbers are built up by both sub-unit and manpower category.

Individual problem areas (e.g. areas of high labour turnover) are pinpointed. If turnover is found to be artificially high in one area or category of employee, the exact causes are investigated and measures are taken to correct/control it, so that it is not reflected as part of the normal pattern of turnover. With accurate figures and the importance attached to the manpower planning process, greater control of manpower is encouraged at all levels of management.

In a business which is labour-intensive, manpower planning has shown the importance of manpower considerations in business planning, in particular the efficient utilization of manpower. By reducing manpower costs to less than forty per cent of sales revenue, it has increased the company's competitiveness. Manpower planning has been a key factor over the past ten years.

Our final chapter will discuss the problem of putting together the various components of human resource management, including manpower planning, to form effective supporting strategies for the commercial and IT challenges of the 1990s.

Further reading

D. J. Bartholemew (Editor), *Manpower Planning* (Penguin, 1976).

D. J. Bell, *Planning Corporate Manpower* (Longman, 1974).

M. Bennison and J. Casson, *The Manpower Planning Handbook* (McGraw Hill, 1983).

J. Bramham, *Practical Manpower Planning* (Institute of Personnel Management, 1982).

C. Purkiss, *Corporate Manpower Planning in the UK*, (Institute of Manpower Studies, 1981).

C. Richards-Carpenter, *Relating Manpower to an Organization's Objectives* (Institute of Manpower Studies, 1982).

A. R. Smith (Editor), *Some Statistical Techniques in Manpower Planning* (HMSO, 1970).

CHAPTER 9

PUTTING EVERYTHING TOGETHER

There is no more important task facing organizations than the development of human resources and the creation of conditions in which those resources can make the fullest use of their abilities.

Paul Darling and Peter Lockwood in *Planning for the Skills Crisis – A Chance to Score.*

Foundations for effective human resource management

It is clear that the major issue in human resource management for information technology is one of skills retention and development, against an apparent insatiable demand for these skills.

The reality of the planning process is examined in this chapter, as are the practical procedures and policies necessary to maximize benefit for both organization and employee.

Planning is more necessary in times of turbulent change

It is a common misconception that planning is impossible when the future is likely to change: the truth is the opposite. Lack of HRM planning in such situations has the potential for disaster.

The principal processes which make good HRM practice are known and accepted. Their application to the management of information technology staff appears problematic and discouraging.

In the early (pioneering) days of commercial computing, to apply such techniques was difficult with no previous patterns, statistics or history to support prediction. More than a quarter of a century later there is no such justification for inactivity.

Case example

A successful multi-national conglomerate, characterized by acquisition and disposal, re-organization, shifting emphasis and constant management change, produces, reviews and implements a five-year information systems plan against a backcloth of continuous commercial surprise.

Within the organization, HRM planning is an integrated corporate process and is well established for the group's international IT community.

A superficial analysis of the fluidity and ambiguity of the organization would provide strong arguments against HRM, yet it is the very dynamism, the constant demand on its managers that proves the case for such a process – a process which views current organization as any pattern in a kaleidoscope: sometimes spectacular, right for the moment, irrelevant when a slight twist in its market or environment dictates a different pattern.

The organization does have HRM problems in its IT areas. However, the problems are clearly identified, analysed, and solutions for both the short and long terms constantly developed.

The group's culture does not allow skills shortage to be an acceptable reason for systems to fail; failure to secure the appropriate human resource does not feature as an option.

This organization has a good track record with its information systems, using technology to improve its market position wherever possible.

The emphasis is on business-driven systems and the improvement of management information for key operational decision-makers across the various business-type boundaries, encouraging the concept of data as a corporate asset (data does not belong to the organization from whose system it was extracted). The continuing need to identify business advantages through the application of information technology is stressed. This emphasis is not dependent upon the prevailing organizational structure which may well change during the five-year period.

The operating companies of the group have systems teams dedicated to their particular business – approximately 700 specialists in total. There is a corporate information technology group providing the technical environment, mainframe and telecommunications facilities, together with support for operating companies' systems teams. Within this corporate specialist resource are high-level business and systems planning experts who assist individual operating companies in the formulation of their systems plans within the Group's five-year programme. The corporate information technology group consists of approximately 150 people, amongst whom are experts who maintain a watching brief on the five-year plan through all the organizational changes which will ensue, assessing the impact of these changes on the plan, and ensuring that the overall direction is not lost.

The 850 specialists form the IT community of the Group, and regular international systems conferences and seminars are held, where personal links are formed with colleagues from other parts of the Group. Opportunities are provided to broaden the understanding of all attendees in terms of other operating companies' development activities.

Individual company systems plans reflect varying levels of development, and degrees of activity in particular application areas. There are clear changes in skills mix over the five-year period.

A major element of the detailed plan is devoted to human resource issues. Although the overall headcount is projected to grow by only one per cent during the five years, the level of internal transfer, training and external recruitment is high. The emphasis on human resource management shows the Group's belief in the importance of planning the skills required to implement its systems strategy and maintain its competitive lead.

Significant HRM points within the plan are:

- Manpower development of IT staff is viewed as a corporate activity and the development review (which includes succession planning, skills audit, and identification of potential) is conducted across all operating companies from junior management upwards. IT is the only group of staff to be managed in this way from a career development point of view. Inputs to this review are business plans, systems strategy and project plans, together with performance appraisal.
- A specialist HRM team exists to facilitate the manpower development of IT staff. The team undertakes corporate IT assignments, but works closely with HRM specialists in the operating companies. It is not intended that this corporate function should replace the activity of operating company HRM teams, indeed any such move would rightly be resisted: the corporate resource should support operating company resources.
- The role of the corporate IT group, as a source of technical skills, is identified and established in the plan. Since the launch of this concept the labour turnover of this team has increased as trained technical staff move to operating companies and trainees are recruited into the corporate team to replace them.
- The emphasis on management information systems, particularly the facilities available with executive workstations and portable terminals, must be supported with proper training for all users. This

training must be thorough and designed to accommodate new users. A corporate trainer is responsible for training and updating individual company trainers who prepare and present their own organizations' programmes, together with common communication systems such as electronic mail.

- A group of multi-discipline graduates are recruited each year for the IT functions. The recruitment process for this graduate intake of approximately twenty per year is organized by the corporate HRM team with the involvement of the operating companies who approve all candidates. The graduates are recruited to join the IT community albeit they will work for a specific operating company. Initial staff and training costs are met by the IT Group: operating companies commence employment responsibility after the initial twelve-week induction and training period. Operating companies are involved in the induction programme and in the creation of learning projects appropriate to their businesses. Graduates on this programme are appraised by the operating companies, but their progress is monitored centrally and transfer around the IT community actively encouraged. The position and immediate future of IT graduates in operating company re-organizations or possible disposals is monitored by the central HRM function, and often swift transfers are effected since the uncertainty of re-organization early on in a career can be destabilizing, resulting invariably in resignation since graduates new to the business environment are often unable to display the maturity to see through a change. Moreover the position of less senior staff tends to be left rather late in the planning process of any re-organized operation.
- The use of technology in training is pursued aggressively. Project teams are evaluating application for expert systems within each operating division. Computer-based training (CBT) modules are an integral part of the design for many new distributed systems. A Group-wide agreement with an external provider makes available a wide range of technical courses, most of which are supported by mainframe computers. PC-based CBT courses include management and personal skills training. The use of this learning technology also widens the confidence of students in the use of terminals and PCs.
- The analysis of likely skills requirements for the five-year period places greater emphasis on personal and managerial skills rather than on specific technical skills training. However, whilst individual technical skills needs will be managed in relation to project schedules, major skills deficiencies are reviewed. Where a Group-wide view showed a strategic need for a particular 4th Generation Language which was new to the UK market, an external consultant was brought in to prepare a training programme. Where possible management

skills courses are used to prepare IT staff who have to interact with non-technical managers. Courses run by external IT training organizations are avoided. The value of in-house management training programmes is greater for IT staff because they interact with managers from their own Group who provide a commercial perspective entirely different from the IT focus.

- All IT vacancies are circulated around the Group to encourage transfer and career growth. The central HRM function, having access to all IT staff development reviews, is able to nominate candidates or identify development assignments for particular individuals.

Where to start and how to keep the HRM cycle moving

We use the HRM schema presented in Chapter 2 as a way of viewing effective management of IT staff. (This is reproduced in Figure 9.1.) By no means revolutionary, the schema merely outlines a modular approach to supporting human resource management for the IT environment.

The basic information required by the procedures and policies noted in the inner circle of the schema will exist within an established organization in varying degrees, although the information may not have been viewed previously from this perspective.

As human resource management is not a precise science – the matter it deals with is individually unpredictable, volatile, and subject to influences outside an employer's control – the absence of a component in the HRM cycle, whilst diluting the benefit will not halt the process from continuing or prevent the cold start-up of the procedures.

Are there links between HRM and the different types of IT strategy? An organization may be using a central computing facility, distributed systems, office automation networks, or end-user systems. The existing IT strategy may be a combination of these approaches. Can these IT environments be supported effectively by one set of HRM procedures and policies? Do the various strategies place different demands on HRM?

We believe there is a basic set of procedures and policies required for all IT environments, but we recognize that the emergence of end-user systems and the supporting IT functions which help end-users to help themselves will place more emphasis on interpersonal skills and training methods.

The inputs required for the HRM system raise many questions

Analysis of performance

Appraisal, assessment of individual performance, obviously provides

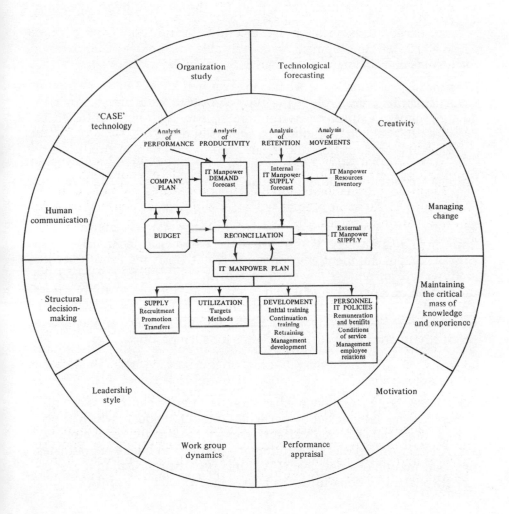

Figure 9.1 The HRM schema Introduced In Chapter 2

significant input to any HRM audit and planning process. But what is the executive board's view of IT performance? Are there shortfalls in the eyes of the end-users? What are the causes of dissatisfaction? What are the expectations within the company plan? What is missing in the performance of the IT team – is this where the problems lie? If so, how is this to be interpreted in the manpower plan for the future? Every question needs to be considered and satisfactory answers given.

Analysis of productivity

Does the organization know what is the required level of productivity for a particular technical role – the unit of output of a programmer in development or support environments? Are the subtle differences between utilization and productivity understood?

Does the organization understand the likely effect of productivity tools, or the introduction of development methodologies – will such aids influence project estimating formulae? When will such changes impact on the organization?

Estimates are a starting point if no other standard exists. Their validity can be monitored and more accurate standards established over time. In the same way, if the difference between a technical role in support or development environments is not clear, the exercise of job analysis will provide a powerful insight into each role, clarifying the proportion of working time which can be related to productivity needs. This will prove a valuable perspective showing why a change in working, perhaps the adoption of a 4GL, will not produce an increase in productivity proportionate to the claims for such products.

Analysis of retention

What is the likely retention rate based on past performance? It is essential to avoid being sidetracked by particular one-off incidents which appear to have drastically affected staff turnover – more 'one-offs' could follow.

Are there any peaks in recruitment – perhaps an intake of graduates, or the formation of a new team? Will this peak be reflected in a proportionate peaking of departures at a later stage from the IT team(s)?

Analysis of movements

Although individuals may remain within the IT organization, the skills and responsibilities will move about. It is important to understand the likely rate of movement away from technical to perhaps supervisory responsibilities, or indeed away from the IT environment completely.

Review of sources for skilled staff

It is important to understand the sources of skill for an organization. Will external events, such as changes in government policy, affect this supply? Many companies in the UK were affected by the reduction in MSC programming courses and the grant aid for training new entrants to IT.

There are many roles in IT functions which grow from other more junior roles. While the flow through this hierarchy continues all is well. However, requirements are modified and consideration should always be given to changes which may be taking place in the source activity or the demand for the developed skills. If there is variation in one without corresponding change in the other, the happy balance collapses.

A case example

A well established bureau had, for a decade or more, dedicated itself to training its own technical operations staff.There was a commitment to an annual intake of school leavers who received thorough training in the fundamentals of data processing with an emphasis on technical operations. The board of the company sanctioned periodic overmanning with trainees, acknowledging that it was impossible to dovetail development of 'green' trainees with the promotion of technical operators possessing two or more years experience. Such trained technicians resourced technical support and systems programming teams as well as other individual roles with a technical bias.

New operational software dramatically reduced the need for technical operators and the annual intake of trainees was scaled down appropriately.

However, the improved operational software did not reduce the need for operations analysts, the demand for their skills being dictated by client support needs. New technical roles were created in specialist support areas to service the new operational software, and the demand for trained technical operations staff therefore continued within the organization, yet the original source had reduced dramatically. Not only was there a resourcing problem, morale and motivation began to suffer also. Demands for the reduced number of experienced technical operators were such that a temporary ban on transfer (and thus promotion) was introduced. The workload demands on the few technical operators became greater, and time available to coach trainees diminished. A negative spiral had come to an organization with a history of enlightened attitudes to IT resourcing, purely through lack of understanding of the true source of the organization's technical staff.

The correction of the problem was a long and costly process. The damage of the decision error was incalculable in terms of morale and the organization's image as a progressive employer providing excellent career prospects.

The possibility of such a situation arising had been gently flagged to the executive responsible for the initial cutback in trainees. There could be no reversal of that decision since immediate cost savings had featured in the justification for the introduction of the operational software. The measurable financial cost of the subsequent resourcing problem outstripped the savings claimed for the next three years!

IT manpower resources inventory

Although common to bureau environments where skills represent an asset, this audit or inventory of IT skills will be a new concept in many other organizations. In most companies, excluding bureaux and software houses, such an inventory will tend to be based on individuals working in an IT function or perhaps a project team of end-users and specialists.

The inventory or audit should be taken both from the perspective of individuals and from skills: skills which currently may not sit in the IT function! The need is to identify all IT manpower resources, specialists and those outside the IT team:

- Look at the managers whose functions have been radicalized by IT. They may be production, distribution or finance experts. These are managers who understand the problems of change. Their expertise will be invaluable in future implementation situations. Their IT skills should be reviewed, they may well have a greater degree of technical awareness than their functional role suggests.
- Consider the young people in the organization. The under-20s will almost certainly have developed keyboard skills and some conceptual understanding of computing, gained from school and home computers.
- Remember the former IT specialists who may have moved into the business itself. Those skills still exist within the organization.
- Consider the end-users. They are familiar with the business and possess specialist knowledge, combined with a growing and probably underestimated knowledge of micro-systems software, etc.

The external IT manpower supply

Before a meaningful and workable IT Manpower Plan can be produced, serious consideration must be given to the labour marketplace. The external IT manpower supply is often viewed as vaguely infinite, providing the asking price is right.

The skills you seek, particularly specific technical experience, are they really available in the market? Where will they be found? Is there a geographic or industry concentration of these skills? Is the demand particularly high at this time? What is known of the success of other recruiters for these skills? There is no point in committing a crucial skills need to recruitment without first researching the chances of real success in the exercise.

The outputs give solutions, but they lead to more questions

The resulting Manpower Plan for IT will set measurable targets, whilst goals will be expressed in policy-type statements.

Supply – recruitment

Recruitment inevitably heads the list when resourcing an IT team. The decision to move into the external supply of manpower is a move into the relatively unknown. However, as with any scarce commodity, external acquisition is possible if an 'at any price' approach is adopted. But this will lead to difficulties with internal equity. Furthermore, the personal motivation of the new recruit has to be questioned. Can the organization meet the individual's needs, and is this role appropriate to the life script of the potential candidate?

The recruitment process for any scarce IT skill will be time consuming and costly, so much careful planning is essential before proceeding (see Appendix 4).

Supply – promotion and transfers

We believe that equal or even greater emphasis should be placed on promotion and transfer. Internal supplies are known and can be quantified accurately – the same confidence does not accompany an expedition into the external market for IT specialists. In planning resources, the promotion or transfer of existing employees should be considered before moving to the external market.

Where job analysis has been conducted there will be a good understanding of the personal qualities and skills required in the role. Care should be taken to recognize the differences in skills requirement between jobs in an apparently logical hierarchy. The job requirements for a senior programmer may include supervision of a small team, and the experience is unlikely to have been gained in the role of a programmer. Whilst training can accelerate the learning process to counteract lack of experience, personal traits will influence how comfortable and effective the individual is in a supervisory role.

There is a tendency to underestimate the capacity of individuals to expand into larger roles and this conservatism may prevent the identification of internal candidates. This is particularly so in the case of trainees who have completed basic skills training. An organization may continue to view them as trainees for an inappropriately long period – many professionals admit to leaving their first employer merely to escape the aura of the young trainee which had continued in some cases for four or five years!

It is an arresting exercise to review the value of trainees and junior staff from the perspective of a new employer, if necessary by constructing CVs. The graduate, who has passed through a company's IT training scheme and had one year's experience as a programmer, is the sought-after two-year professional in the eyes of a predator organization. The straight-from-school trainee who has worked in network control for a year – probably doing a lot of photocopying and clerical tasks in that time – is a network controller in the eyes of a recruiting organization, particularly where the predator is new to the particular communications hardware. The secretary responsible for introducing new administrative personnel to the office utility systems has the potential to be considered an end-user trainer by another company.

If other organizations will risk appointing young and apparently short-experienced recruits, then surely the current employers with their more detailed knowledge of the individual are able to take a more calculated risk.

We never cease to be amazed by the proportion of young professionals who make their first move on to the external market due to lack of recognition by their employers, especially as these companies have invested heavily in their initial training. Due recognition of their worth is expected to be shown in a mix of remuneration and attitudes of peers and supervisors. They are aware of improvements in their own performance and seek instantaneous recognition, failing to understand that employers have recruited them in a raw state in anticipation of such growth. Astute managers will recognize this situation and pay due regard to these issues in appraisal and other counselling situations.

Utilization

The effective application of skills to the business needs is an accepted commercial aim, but there is a different perspective which is often overlooked. As we have seen in earlier chapters, dedicated employees are likely to work harder for long hours when the organization provides appropriate challenges and the motivation of all involved is high. A contributing factor to continuing motivation will be the value or worth put on individual efforts. Individuals must never feel that their efforts have been ineffective due to poor management of a task.

When people work overnight to unravel a problem they will be exhausted, but recognition of their efforts – not necessarily material, often a word from an appropriate executive – will complete their satisfaction. The 'often' does not apply to the frequency of such situations. If the muddle recurs, and the overnight stint becomes the accepted way of life, irrespective of the verbal bouquets or even generous ex gratia payments, staff tolerance will vanish and earlier satisfaction of team effort will not apply. Where extra effort is required from IT employees, such dedication should not be abused. Staff will feel they are being exploited, rather than management facing up to the cost of rewriting an existing application which constantly collapses.

It is not enough to set completion targets for projects or tasks: the structuring of project development, or the organization of support, must take into account the need of individuals to achieve. Whilst this makes sound commonsense, the result of failure is not only unnecessary cost, but more disastrously, the disenchantment of the skilled employee.

If a system of performance-related pay is employed in the organization which operates as a meritocracy, merit and performance must be measurable, and not left to subjective judgment alone. We examined in earlier chapters the setting of goals, targets, and levels of performance. Tom Philp[1] argues against the *the role is nebulous* syndrome used by some managers who are against setting performance standards. Obviously, numeric measures cannot apply to all roles, nonetheless without some understanding of the quantitive or qualitative capacity of a role, how can any evaluation be made?

Whilst the scarcity of IT skills is an important issue, it is alarming how skills can be wasted through poor management of time. Great effort must be made to plan the best usage of these expensive skills: inconvenient office layouts, lack of terminals, ill-planned testing time, badly maintained technical libraries, lack of administrative support, even chaos in the car park, all take their toll on time.

Development – management and staff

The development of IT staff is, as with many technical specialists, misleadingly termed *management development*.

Not all technologists make good managers, project or functional. Those who are successful in a project environment, as managers of large teams, do not necessarily find fulfilment in an ongoing functional role. However, the development of IT staff is a major contributor to retention. An individual presented with a development target and plan, given the opportunity to attend non-technical skills training, sees acknowledgement of his/her individuality, rather than the exploitation of his/her technical skills.

In succession planning, target roles should be identified so that qualities and skills required in a real post form the basis of training plans. It would be ingenuous to imagine that such target roles will ever be attained in the form first identified, since change will influence the shape of that role over time.

Target roles should not be confined to IT functions. IT specialists should be considered for roles within main business streams, other administrative or support functions. It should never be assumed that specialists should stay within their original field. As personal needs change with maturity, employers must strive to understand the individual's need for fulfilment. Unexpected decisions by IT professionals to 'opt out' during mid career are indicative of this lack of fulfilment.

At less senior levels, care should be taken to identify the qualities of roles seen to fall into a logical hierarchy. If the inter-relationship of these roles appears less logical from the skills perspective, the step by step development of individuals should not be abandoned. Care taken to introduce proper training in support of these new demands, and enlightened monitoring of performance, will support any joint decisions to think again or proceed. Where personal needs and demands of a role are not perfectly matched, yet business demands may require the role to be filled, the situation can be viewed as a career development assignment.

Job analysis will present a role as a collection/group of tasks requiring a sometimes surprisingly wide range of skills: to see a job as the handling of one task is a widely established misunderstanding of the nature of jobs in IT.

But can it be assumed that all IT personnel (managers, specialists and end-users) are motivated to develop and face the prospect of change? Obviously, this cannot be the case. Technicians often lack the courage to take development steps, claiming to be interested in technical matters only. In the highly specialist areas – systems programming, sizing, and network design – this is music to the ears of many a manager attempting to keep the IT boat afloat. The skills are in short supply, so just leave the competent technical expert in his potting shed! But there are dangers if there is no gradual modification in stance. A block may be created for the development of more junior specialists, a 'prima donna' may be created, and the organization becomes vulnerable through its reliance on an individual. Apparent stability is gained at the expense of not disseminating technical knowledge. This is not skills retention – skill has become a hostage, and there is potential for blackmail.

Development – appraisal

Appraisal, the formal documentation of what should be a normal natural interaction between managers and their staff, is a major input to the IT personnel development process. The procedures, whilst measuring performance in a current role and defining actions for performance improvement, must seek to evaluate the individual's contribution to the business need (the value added).

Whilst appraisal has a retrospective aspect, the true objective is to improve the performance of the individual, and in turn the organization, by identifying strengths and weaknesses which will influence future career development and performance. Likewise, organizational issues which can constrain individual achievement must be identified. If appraisal is to be an effective tool, it must be a process jointly owned, with appraisee and appraiser contributing and gaining from the interchange. In times of change, when creative personal qualities are essential, the value of the ongoing appraisal process (constant feedback and encouragement by managers) should be recognized. Appraisal must not be an annual bureaucratic process. To be successful, the approach must be a positive and valued process which enhances individual development and performance. It has to be an integral part of every manager's repertoire of people skills.

Development – training

Management training must be introduced into IT staff training plans, in the same way that appropriate IT courses should be available to business managers. IT personnel need to understand the business they serve, as well as their organizations' short and long-term objectives.

Technical conversion training should be an accepted element of the training budget/activity, to be utilized by existing and new employees.

Training for the end-user environment must be a continuous process. All new staff in such areas need to receive immediate training to acquaint them with the day-to-day operation and potential of the systems. Many end-user systems are now designed to include CBT (computer-based training) modules. But the intervention of a trainer or supervisor is still of great value to ensure learning has been achieved and encourage exploitation of the facilities provided.

Many small organizations have committed funds to IT based on multiple PCs. These systems (hardware, software, and the human resources) represent major investments in proportion to the size of the companies. It is not uncommon to discover that adequate training, other than during the installation of hardware, does not take place. New employees are left to read badly-written manuals or to learn from their colleagues who have no concept of training methods or the learning process. The need for training in such operations must be recognized, the responsibility allocated to specific individuals, and progress monitored. Such individuals require training for the responsibilities. In a small organization this cannot be achieved internally, but there are many suitable 'Train the Trainer' programmes provided by external training companies. Local education establishments provide courses on basic products, word processing, database, and spreadsheets. Local networks of small employers or trade associations may have some support to offer.

In the medium to large-scale companies, end-user systems generate similar problems, but they are overcome by the professional activities of

Information Centre personnel who are charged with the responsibility of helping end-users to help themselves.

IT personnel policies – general

Whilst most components of the IT manpower plan must accommodate adjustment and change, personnel policies must be more enduring, though malleable. The courage to establish and adhere to HRM policies for the IT environment is critical, since events and short-term problems will attempt to destabilize the human resources.

Remuneration policies

It is a peculiarity of pay and benefits structures that expensive benefits can become costly demotivators. This applies in all areas of employment, and is to be found in the IT environment.

Remuneration practice for IT personnel must:

- Recognize the salary growth profile of an IT career (see Figure 9.2).
- Be based on a published salary policy.
- Interface with the packages for other professionals.
- Facilitate rather than hinder, transfers in and out of the IT specialism.
- Provide a sensible balance between order and flexibility.

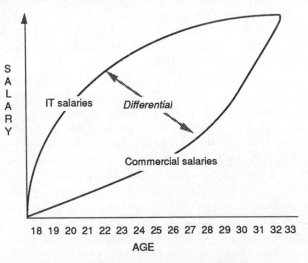

Figure 9.2 Salary growth – comparison between commercial and IT personnel

- Prevent distortion of the basic: variable earnings ratios, which can produce inaccurate perceptions of value of a job, as well as preventing transfer to other roles, and a disincentive to improve operational efficiency.
- Consider inconvenience and disturbance allowances of equal value irrespective of grade or base salary. Percentage allowances should be discouraged since they grow in value with seniority and become a barrier to development.

Such propositions may be unrealistic in those organizations where the remuneration practice of an entire industry must include the IT component. However, IT staff generally receive higher base salaries than other staff on shift or call, and belong to a grouping which is expected to develop rapidly. Therefore, the impact of the loss of variable earnings or shift allowances can be more acute.

The integration of IT staff remuneration with the rest of the organization is much debated: 'red circling', special skills supplements, distortion (drift) within job evaluation scales are possible reactions, if not solutions to the problem. The evolving end-user systems environment, combined with the gradual blurring of boundaries between IT specialists, managers and other professionals from different disciplines, must influence the decision to follow any such route since the resulting actions will have an impact over a far wider area than in the past. Furthermore there is evidence that the 'specialness' of these skills is diminishing as the glamour or mystery of IT evaporates.

Conditions of service

Conditions of service are often expressions of management/employee relations. Where there is a strong organizational culture, this is likely to be positively assimilated in the end-user environment, but the more technically orientated IT staff may be impervious to it.

Conditions of service cannot be tailored to one work group, particularly when that group is a small service team removed from the 'mother' industry or business. However, it is important to understand the likely reaction of this group to changes which might be welcomed by other groups. An example is the approach to hours of work. A flexible approach to working hours may be the necessary way of working for some IT staff. The introduction of time recording devices to support a formal system of flexible working may at best be constraining, but could well produce an attitude of time watching, previously absent in the professional IT environment.

Management/employee relations

The relationship of IT staff with their host company may be uncomfortable due to the lack of understanding about viewpoint, objectives, and ways of working. There is much potential for conflict in the IT environment, and the level of stress will increase if appropriate human resource management strategies are not developed.

Struggles over limited hard and soft resources, the independent attitude of IT technical specialists, and faulty interpersonal relationships, can lead to levels of conflict which damage all parties. If conflict is mishandled it can be completely negative, resulting in poor communication and below optimum utilization of human resources.

Most commercial managers are keen to improve the performance of their own responsibility areas. This may include increased usage of information technology. But poor relationships with the IT function(s) may cause them to be over-anxious about the future end-user systems. They often feel that making a move into a new area of IT can be likened to the prospect of a parachute jump! The closer they come to the event, the more anxious they become. Anxiety leads to stress, and stress will lead inevitably to conflict situations. An IT specialist may not always understand, or have internalized the experience of using an on-line application with phones ringing, constant noise, bad lighting, and a screen layout designed to demand eye acrobatics to follow a string of required information. The end-user managers are well aware of the difficulties, but find they are unable to communicate their concern to the IT specialist without appearing to be reactionary. The situation becomes more and more frustrating, and eventually an explosion of conflict will take place.

The various sub-cultures and tribal languages which exist within every company, including the areas of information technology and human resource management, guarantee misunderstandings about the motives behind various actions. Conflict is partly due to difficulties of interacting with personnel from other sub-cultures, who follow different rules, use different psychological signal systems, and have different ideas.

Skillful negotiation will be paramount in the emerging information technology environment of the 1990s. 'Getting to Yes' between multiple representatives who are in conflict will make heavy demands on commercial, IT, and human resource management executives. The CEOs will be expected to steer these negotiators towards a problem-solving approach and arrive at a solution which is workable and acceptable to all parties.

But these agreements could be undermined by other personnel involved in implementing corporate strategies – commercial, IT, and human resource management. Therefore, it is essential to develop cooperative and participative involvement of staff in these strategies if they are to be implemented successfully. We recognize this concept may not be greeted with favour by those managers who believe in the X management style. However, we believe that successful application of information technology is dependent on good relations between management and employees. A dictatorial style associated with information technology strategies is a recipe for disaster – good news for all the consultancies who make a living out of clearing up IT messes, but bad news for those executives responsible for maximizing corporate performance.

The next steps in the way forward

In this chapter we have moved quickly from what might seem to be a sophisticated procedure removed from daily pressures to the real and practical components which make up the planning process for IT human resources. The appendices contain guidelines to support this approach.

Many readers will come from organizations where one or more of these processes will not seem relevant. Others may not have the data available in suitable format. The size of the company may not justify job evaluation, and formal job descriptions may seem alien to a small group.

Tom Peters, in his book *Thriving on Chaos*, advocates the abandonment of job descriptions in his mission to make managers and their businesses more sensitive to their markets. He believes they should be making a positive response to the changing business environment around them, rather than concentrating on their current job descriptions. But evaluation of the relative worth of various roles, and their interrelationships within the organization, based on agreed value factors, does require some formal description of the role!

Job evaluation provides justification for pay structure and lessens the damaging subjectivity of unpopular differentials. However, the more powerful process which proceeds evaluation is *job analysis*, the key to making other HRM processes effective and relevant to the IT environment, particularly the planning of training and development.

We believe there is misunderstanding of the real content of IT roles, and this may account for the inertia relating to the human resource issues. Speak to the job holders, listen to their descriptions of a typical day. Discover the true nature of the technical role. Establish the relevance of numeracy in a development role, examine the physical demands made on network support staff, understand the need for keyboard skills in end-user environments, determine the scope for disaster and its impact on the business of the lone operator on the weekend night shift. Identify what use is made of rare and costly technical skills – are they fully exploited in specific technical roles?

The process of job analysis, as a bold step in understanding the nature of IT jobs or geared to job evaluation, can produce apparent misconceptions about roles. Do not be alarmed if the process produces strange results. Examine them before dismissing them – they may contain pointers for a different way of resourcing a particular role.

As the process continues, career development links should be sought, accepted career paths should be questioned. Are the qualities of an excellent programmer the same for an analyst or a team leader? Are the skills of an accounts assistant using a terminal similar to an applications systems support role? Do the skills exercised by junior draughtsmen using CAD techniques and working in a modern design office have connections with expert systems?

In an environment where career development is an accepted feature of the organizational culture, job holders, when presented with the prospect of their own promotion, willingly discuss the skills and qualities required in their successor, together with the type of training required. When an environment instils confidence rather than suspicion of management's motives, the concept of preparing a person specification for your successor will be seen as commitment to moving forward, not a threat to the security of current roles. Such cultures are not created overnight, neither do they require a decade to establish. Consistent and determined HRM activities steaming ahead while reorganizations, crisis and change threaten the path, will give evidence of commitment to the organization's long-term intention to develop, not exploit, to plan rather than panic, and will remarkably quickly produce a change in attitude.

The HRM cycle for the IT environment has to start somewhere, even if it means managers 'push-starting' the process. If management is reticent, why does it hesitate? The future will contain many challenges, so the fear of change must be overcome. Technical complexity or the mystique of IT and HRM must not be allowed to stand in the way.

Darling and Lockwood[2] concentrate on the pressure to introduce HRM techniques in the advent of the demographic issue and particularly the early 1990s dip. They express serious concern at the apparent apathy towards the impending crisis, whilst commending the steps of the few organizations who are facing the next decade with eyes open and plans well established. They identify IT amongst the activities most likely to affect adversely the performance of companies and indeed whole industries due to skill shortage.

We have not suggested that any one aspect of the approach to HRM in the information technology environment is a panacea, other than to plan despite uncertainty. Without a plan there is no action, only reaction to events. A plan can be created, imperfect maybe through lack of data, but none the less a plan against which events can be monitored. The plan for IT human resources should include individual career development proposals, and allow staff to see themselves as individuals, yet part of a total strategy. These IT human resources must not be seen as a source of skills currently in demand but expendable as circumstances change. The objective must be to maintain the critical mass of knowledge and experience.

The current and predicted skill shortages are prompting organizations new to HRM planning to ponder their future in the light of this problem. Planning for the human resources is rapidly becoming recognized as an essential process in many organizations who previously managed to survive without. However, because HRM planning for the information technology environment is so critical to all organizations, it must not be embraced as a peripheral activity or consigned vaguely to managers responsible for IT. In this book we have examined the HRM processes which provide the 'how'. But the real challenge is 'to make it happen'. As Sir John Harvey-Jones stresses,[3] individuals need to be charged with responsibility, in this case for HRM, then left to develop their own tactics (no doubt incorporating many of the ideas and approaches we have touched on in this book) to make planning for the human resource in the information technology environment a reality.

Notes and references

1   Tom Philp, *Making Performance Appraisal Work* (McGraw-Hill, 1983).
2   Philip Darling and Peter Lockwood, *Planning for the Skills Crisis – A Chance to Score* (Institute of Personnel Management, 1988).
3   Sir John Harvey-Jones, *Making it Happen – Reflections on Leadership* (Collins, 1988).

BACKGROUND RESEARCH METHODOLOGY

Introduction

The gestation period for this book has lasted exactly five years, but the joint professional experience of the writers and those colleagues associated with supporting the research project amounted to well over one hundred man/woman years working in the information technology, management development, training, personnel management, recruitment and consultancy spheres.

The practical background of the team has influenced our approach to the complex and challenging topics of human resource management and information technology. Throughout the whole process of research, discussion and writing this book, we were determined to ensure that our activities would lead towards one specific objective – to assist and encourage corporate management faced with developing appropriate human resource management strategies for the information technology environment(s) of the 1990s. There has been no attempt to produce an academic or generalized statement about the problems. Each phase of our work was designed to ensure we did not ignore the day-to-day practical difficulties faced by managers.

The initial research assignment consisted of four phases:

- A preliminary survey of information technology and human resource management in a sample group of companies.

- A review of the survey findings, followed by detailed discussions with a range of the companies.
- A further survey of a second sample group of companies.
- An assessment of findings from the first three phases, leading to the publication of a preliminary report.

Survey phases

The two confidential surveys, each of six months, included a wide variety of business and commercial sectors:

Furniture manufacturing
High technology
Advanced instrumentation manufacturing
Life assurance
Banking
Retailing (food and household goods)
Protective clothing services
Paper goods manufacturing
Book publishing
Local government
Pharmaceutical manufacturing
Financial services
DIY and industrial tools manufacturing
Regional health authorities
International airlines
Automotive products manufacturing and distribution.

In addition to these sectors, the third phase included members of several professional associations directly associated with human resource management and information technology.

Both surveys were based on questionnaires distributed to a total of 250 companies – seventy per cent of these companies agreed to participate.

The questionnaires were organized into four parts:

Part 1: general information about corporate attitudes towards human resource management (including responding to change, harmonization of rewards, training, re-training, and performance appraisal).
Part 2: questions relating to strategic planning (time horizons, depth of planning, and the level of integration between planning for information technology, human resource management, and corporate commercial objectives).

Part 3: questions relating to organizational study (co-ordinated studies by personnel management and information technology specialists).

Part 4: questions relating to human resource management planning and information technology activities (performance appraisal, job enrichment, succession/career planning, education/training, skills analysis, remuneration structures and recruitment policies).

The format of the questionnaires allowed participants to select from multiple choice answers to each question. The participants were also given the opportunity to comment further on all questions.

Research findings and this book

The preliminary findings from the first phase suggested that additional discussions should take place with approximately forty companies spread across the sixteen sectors.

As the companies participating in the research have different perceptions and practical experience of human resource management and information technology, no attempt has been made by the writers or the research team to produce a sector 'league table' because such an exercise would be misleading.

The research findings suggested that any book addressing the topics of human resource management and information technology would have to:

- Define the link between human resource management and information technology (evaluating performance and improving jobs; planning succession, careers, education and training; making the most of available skills; recruiting IT personnel; and the HRM/IT schema).
- Make the appropriate connection between strategic planning and information technology.
- Help managers understand and prepare for change.
- Develop management's understanding of 'knowledge transfer' and 'maintaining the critical mass of experience/skills'.
- Comment on the common failure to recognize motivational patterns and life scripts.
- Link performance appraisal, leadership, work group behaviour, decision making, communications, and information technology, to improvements in utilization and productivity.
- Explain, through a practical example, manpower planning concepts.
- Bring together and discuss the various components which form an effective approach to human resource management in the information technology environment(s) of the 1990s.

General introduction

Our experience in personnel management and consultancy suggests that HRM audit of the IT environment leads to major improvements in terms of availability, productivity, and utilization of IT skills.

The preliminary audit approach we suggest in this Appendix follows the format of the HRM/IT schema discussed in Chapters 2 and 9. The schema should not be thought of as a 'hard system'. It is a conceptual way of viewing the role of HRM and supporting activities in the IT environments of the 1990s.

Plans which support investments in IT manpower (managers, technical specialists and end-users) should provide a framework within which it is possible to contain the labour costs and improve productivity of IT skills. The majority of management actions are short term, all within the one-year financial budget period. This may be the first period of the IT manpower plan and its shape should be related to the longer-term forecast for corporate requirements. It must stand by itself as the platform from which campaigns for controlling the costs of information technology skills are launched.

However, financial budgets in themselves cannot ensure that corporate commercial/IT objectives and goals are achieved. These budgets cannot analyse systems requirements, maintain effective project management or implement the new advanced information technology. It is possible for an IT financial budget to look acceptable when in reality the actual performance of the corporate IT investment is not good.

One problem with financial budgets for IT is the level of confidence which can be placed in the figures representing skills, both numbers and costs. There are a variety of reasons for this:

- An IT budget is a forecast and therefore subject to all the weaknesses of any decisions dependent on future corporate scenarios rich with changes.
- An IT budget manager has imprecise information to assess future costs. The management tools at his/her disposal to estimate the number of analysts and programmers, database specialists, Information Centre and systems software support personnel may be inadequate, if they exist at all.
- The human factor – managers may feel threatened by financial budgets, especially when they are used as techniques for coercion rather than positive aids to planning and controlling IT skills and costs.

Managers are tempted to put in a 'fudge factor' for IT skills believing numbers and costs will always be cut back. Senior corporate executives who review IT budgets understand all about fudge factors – they have participated in the game themselves – and will automatically reduce budgets to eliminate fudge. This misuse of budgeting undermines any attempt to solve the problems of IT skills shortages.

Financial budgets for IT skills may be correct at the time of preparation, but how does corporate management ensure that these budgets continue to be valid? Commercial and technical circumstances change, and if the IT budgets are wrong, which unfortunately does happen, change will compound the errors.

Finally, there is the problem of using the financial budgets. Do the budgets for IT skills control numbers and costs, or do they tend to become academic exercises generating lengthy reports which are largely ignored? Does the information in the financial budgets enable management to identify IT skills problems?

The essential components of an IT manpower plan

An effective IT Manpower Plan should be prepared on the basis of an analysis of skills requirements and a study of the implications for their utilization, productivity and costs. The main elements, depending on circumstances, should include:

Recruitment Plan – the numbers and types of IT skills needed and when they are required; any special supply problems and how they are to be dealt with; the detailed recruitment programme.

Personnel Redevelopment Plan – activities for retraining existing employees in the required IT skills.

Redundancy Plan – given IT skills which are no longer required, who is to be made redundant, where and when; the plans for redevelopment or retraining, where this has not been covered in the redevelopment plan; the steps to be taken to help redundant employees find new jobs; the policy for declaring redundancies and making redundancy payments.

Training Plan – the number of IT skills required and the programme for recruiting or training existing personnel in them; the courses to be developed or the changes to be made to existing courses.

Productivity Plan – the programme for improving utilization and productivity of IT skills (streamlining development methods using 4GLs or CASE tools; improved project management techniques; technology-based training procedures; and developing other methods of improving motivation and commitment: organization development programmes, redesigning jobs, and increased participation).

Retention Plan – the actions required to reduce avoidable wastage of IT skills (pay problems; IT specialists and end-users leaving to further their careers: providing better career opportunities; extending opportunities for training; adopting and implementing 'promotion from within' policies and introducing more systematic and equitable promotion procedures; employees leaving because of conflict: introducing more effective procedures for consultation, participation, and handling of grievances; improving communication between groups and individuals; reorganizing work methods and office space to increase group cohesiveness; helping commercial management, IT specialists and end-users to improve their relationships).

In each of the six areas of the IT manpower plan it is necessary to estimate the skills in terms of numbers and costs involved, and relate them to the potential benefits. It will also be necessary to indicate who is responsible for implementing the plan, for reporting on progress and for monitoring the results achieved.

Structure of the audit

Before embarking on the development of HRM policies and manpower planning procedures for the IT environment, we recommend a preliminary audit which allows for a global view of the current situation. The structure of the audit follows the format of the HRM/IT schema, and is divided into three phases:

• A review of the *outer circle* activities (organization study, technological forecasting, creativity, change management, maintaining the critical mass of knowledge and experience, motivation, performance appraisal, work group dynamics, leadership style, structured decision-making, human formal and informal communication, and 'CASE' technology).

- A review of the *inner circle* activities (manpower planning in general, demand forecasting, supply forecasting, current action plans, benefits and problems).
- The identification of areas within IT requiring HRM action.

Any attempt to speed up the audit process by avoiding any of the phases or questions will reduce its overall effectiveness.

Phase 1 – review of the outer circle activities

SECTION A – ORGANIZATIONAL STUDY:

1   Given that information technology is now available for most business areas, to what extent are the Personnel and IT functions jointly studying the implications for organizational development?
2   How are major disagreements resolved between different parts of the organization where information systems cross traditional lines of control and responsibility?
3   How are conflicts resolved between those who develop information systems and those who have to use them to assist in the achievement of corporate commercial objectives?
4   Is organizational study included within the education plans for corporate managers? If so, in what way?
5   Have corporate managers recently reviewed the problems associated with centralization and specialization? What were their conclusions?

SECTION B – TECHNOLOGICAL FORECASTING:

1   Is the company a member of any IT research organization? Which one?
2   Has the company benefited from the analysis of technological trends by the research organization? In what way?
3   Does the company use technological forecasting techniques as part of its own strategic planning procedures? What methods are used?

SECTION C – CREATIVITY:

1   What is done to ensure that creative ability exists at all levels of the organization?
2   How is creative potential identified in each person?

3 Do the existing job specifications include a determination of the required creativity levels? How are these levels defined?
4 Is the development of creativeness a topic within the corporate education and training programmes? What is the approach to the subject?

SECTION D – CHANGE MANAGEMENT:

1 Does change just happen in a random fashion, or is it managed? In what way is it managed?
2 How are the cultural, social, organizational and psychological aspects of resisting change identified in the company?
3 Are management failing to listen and respond to questions about job security? If so, why is this?

SECTION E – MAINTAINING THE CRITICAL MASS OF
KNOWLEDGE AND EXPERIENCE:

1 How does the company maintain the existing critical mass of knowledge and experience, especially IT skills?
2 Is the transfer of knowledge part of the corporate commercial strategies? How is this achieved?
3 How are the training needs of the individual and the organization co-ordinated?

SECTION F – MOTIVATION:

1 How does the company motivate its IT employees (managers, technical specialists, and end-users)?
2 What part do the classical theories of motivation play in the development and management of IT employees?
3 To what extent are job design, task restructuring and job enrichment programmes part of corporate strategies?
4 How are the personality, character, and talents of each IT employee harnessed to the strategic needs of the organization?

SECTION G – PERFORMANCE APPRAISAL:

1 What is the executive board's view of IT performance?
2 Are there shortfalls in IT performance in the eyes of the end-users? If so, what are they?
3 What are the causes of these shortfalls and dissatisfaction with IT performance?
4 Is each IT employee (manager, technical specialist, and end-user) regularly appraised in terms of individual performance?
5 How are the potential negative aspects of performance appraisal avoided?

6   How are the performance appraisal procedures monitored?
7   How are the performance standards agreed?

SECTION H – WORK GROUP DYNAMICS:

1   How are IT work groups developed in the company?
2   Is the topic of 'work group dynamics' included in the management education and training programme? If so, in what way?
3   How does the company combat role ambiguity?

SECTION I – LEADERSHIP STYLE:

1   Is leadership style in the IT environment considered to be a crucial issue by the company? How are the required styles identified?
2   Do leaders just emerge within the company, or are they developed?
3   Do the medium and long-term commercial and IT strategic plans suggest the need to develop different styles of leadership?

SECTION J – STRUCTURED DECISION-MAKING:

1   Are managers trained in structured decision-making?
2   To what extent does 'satisficing' operate in the acquisition of IT skills from internal and external labour markets?
3   How are IT work groups involved in structured decision-making?

SECTION K – FORMAL AND INFORMAL COMMUNICATIONS:

1   Is training in interpersonal and communication skills given to all IT workers (managers, technical specialists, and end-users)? What form does this training take?
2   How are effective communication procedures established when structuring IT projects and work groups?

SECTION L – CASE TECHNOLOGY:

1   Are structured systems development methodologies used in the IT function(s)?
2   To what extent are 4GLs and CASE technology utilized by the company?
3   What plans exist for training the end-users to use these systems development tools?

Phase 2 – review of the inner circle activities

SECTION A – GENERAL QUESTIONS ON MANPOWER
PLANNING

1 Does the company operate a manpower planning procedure? Does it include the IT function(s)?
2 What is the status accorded to the manpower planning function?
3 What importance is attached to the manpower planning procedure?
4 In what way is the organization's IT manpower planning associated with business planning?
5 How comprehensive is the manpower planning procedure? Does it include all geographical sites and all categories of manpower?
6 Is the procedure standardized throughout the organization?
7 To what extent are computing facilities used in the procedure?
8 When was the current procedure for manpower planning introduced?
9 What system or procedure did it replace?
10 Why was manpower planning introduced?
11 How was the system introduced?
12 What problems, if any, were experienced in introducing the procedure?
13 How specifically is manpower planning associated with manpower costs?
14 Are there any overall cost constraints on IT manpower?
15 How are IT manpower budgets decided?
16 How accurately are current IT labour costs known?
17 How accurately are future IT labour costs predicted?
18 Over what time scale does the IT manpower plan operate?
19 How easily can the plan react to changes in company policy and adjustments to the forecast?

SECTION B – IT DEMAND FORECASTING

1 How is IT manpower requirement related to activity levels of the company?
2 To what extent is IT manpower requirement linked to current levels of manpower or independent of current levels?
3 To what extent does zero-based budgeting operate within the IT function(s)?
4 Does IT manpower investment have to compete with alternative forms of investment in achieving targets?
5 How is the IT demand forecast adjusted in the light of anticipated organizational, technological, or social changes?
6 How far are IT productivity and utilization considerations taken into account in predicting demand?

7   How much managerial discretion is retained in estimating IT demand?
8   What processes contribute to IT demand forecasting?
9   How is the IT demand forecast finally decided?
10 How detailed is the breakdown of the IT demand forecast?
11 What system of classification of IT manpower (manpower category) is used?
12 What is the length of the IT demand forecasting cycle?
13 What are the main problems for the organization in forecasting IT demand?

SECTION C – IT SUPPLY FORECASTING

1   How far does an accurate picture of current IT manpower stock exist?
2   How comprehensive is the data held for each IT employee, including historical data?
3   Is the data available centrally or dispersed?
4   Is the data uniformly available?
5   To what extent is the data available and in a form suitable for IT supply forecasting?
6   What computerized system, if any, of IT supply forecasting is used?
7   What factors are taken into account in IT supply forecasting – internal and external?
8   How is IT labour turnover measured and analysed?
9   Are any other 'flows' examined which affect IT supply forecasting?
10 What is the length of the IT supply forecasting cycle?
11 How accurate is IT supply forecasting?
12 What problems are encountered in IT supply forecasting?

SECTION D – CURRENT ACTION PLANS

1   Who is responsible for translating the results of the IT manpower forecasts into HRM policies?
2   What action plans are developed from the IT forecast figures?
3   How significant is the turnover rate, and does it play a part in achieving IT manpower targets?
4   Does the organization experience IT shortages or surpluses?
5   What measures has the organization developed to overcome forecast IT shortages or surpluses?

SECTION E – BENEFITS AND PROBLEMS

1   What benefits has the organization obtained from its IT manpower planning system? Can they be improved?
2   Has manpower planning contributed to better utilization of IT manpower and greater control of IT manpower costs?

3 How effective is manpower planning for assisting career development of IT employees (managers, technical specialists and end-users)?
4 Is the information produced from the IT manpower forecasts in the form management require, is it significant, is it used?
5 How do IT line management and unions view the manpower planning process?
6 Has the organization evaluated the contribution made by IT manpower planning to corporate profitability?

Phase 3 – the identification of potential HRM/IT action areas

1 What improvements are required in the IT manpower database?
2 What action is required to set up IT manpower planning procedures where none exists at present?
3 What needs to be done to improve the effectiveness of existing IT manpower planning procedures?
4 What needs to be done to improve the existing budgeting aspects of manpower planning?
5 If a study of IT productivity trends suggests that productivity is low, what is to be done about it?
6 Does the analysis of IT manpower trends/ratios and of productivity indices suggesting overmanning in any area? If so, what is to be done about it?
7 Does the organization and planning of IT projects lead to irregular flows of work, idle time or under-use of IT personnel?
8 Is sufficient attention paid by IT management to the labour saving potential of investment in new hardware and software?
9 Are all levels of IT management, supervision and personnel adequately motivated?
10 Is there scope for improving the efficiency and/or reducing the cost (without impairing efficiency) of recruitment, induction training, continuation training, and management development of IT personnel?
11 Is there any friction in the relationships between IT departments causing poor communications, delays or inefficiencies?
12 Has sufficient account been taken of the likely resistance to any proposed changes in manpower planning systems and procedures for the IT function(s)?
13 Have steps been taken to give responsibility for improving the utilization and productivity of IT skills to a senior director or IT executive?

As information technology becomes more integral to the operation of the business, the necessity for management to consider the impact on human resources grows. In many companies the repercussion on IT skills is either considered minimal or not considered at all.

Whilst HRM is not an integral part of many managers' thinking, the HRM plan is as crucial as the financial budget - more so, in that cash is more infinite than people!

What are the decisions, the situations, the trigger points which will affect the HRM plan? When should the plan be subject to unscheduled review? We would draw your attention to the following 'triggers' for action:

- New products/services.
- Change of location.
- Acquisition/disposal.
- Technological developments.
- Systems policy changes.
- Legislative changes.
- Market forces.
- Demographic issues.
- National/international politics.
- New missions/core values.
- Reorganization/job re-structuring.

RECRUITMENT CHECKLIST

Preparation of a recruitment assignment must be thorough and comprehensive if it is to be successful. Yet it is often neglected or given superficial attention. A checklist for the recruitment strategy, including the job and person specifications, should cover:

- Numbers required.
- Timescale.
- Alternative strategies.
- What are the tasks/projects/roles?
- What qualities are required of the potential candidate?
- What type of experience is sought?
- Is the potential candidate to be leader, team member, co-ordinator?
- Application or industry.
- Hardware or software.

The job and person specifications must always be subject to initial challenge and the minimum 'essential' technical criteria established with other personal and technical needs classified as 'desirable'.

Seasoned recruiters in IT will confirm that invariably the satisfactory conclusion of a difficult recruitment will involve some compromise on the original specifications. Sometimes the process is extended over a lengthy period, and influences the value of compromise. In other cases, the candidate's presentation at the interviews will convince the selector despite the lack of exact match with defined requirements - particularly technical experience.

HRM specialists working with IT professionals will often comment on the following phenomenon. Presented with a CV, tangible qualities will be tested against the specifications, and rejected where a clear match does not exist, data being compared with data. The rejection process is not so clear-cut when a potential candidate is put in front of a manager. IT professionals are not alone in this tendency, engineers and other technologists behave in the same way during the selection process.

A common requirement is for experience of a specific duration, for example two years. Such a specific need requires the recruiter to play the role of being a crackshot who must shoot the target at a particular point in career growth. Over a six-month recruitment campaign there is twenty-five per cent variation in this precise criterion.

The specifications demand answers to a range of questions:

- Do you really mean precisely what you say?
- If not, how far are you prepared to compromise?
- What if the potential candidates cannot be found at the price you can afford, what is the fallback?
- What will be the effect on the business if recruitment does not succeed?

Where significant numbers of specific groups are required, there has to be room for variation from the tight specification. For example, if there is a six-month period in which to recruit eighteen analyst/programmers with experience of a certain 4GL, conversion training of otherwise suitable candidates should be considered and actioned at the outset of the campaign. Similarly, where time permits, recruitment from thick sandwich courses, graduates and HND students should not be discounted.

There may be problems should the numbers of those recruited represent a significant proportion of existing headcount. Where the proportion is more than thirty per cent, management must understand the difficulties associated with assimilating the newcomers into the existing work group. The possible effect on existing personnel, specialists and in-house developed trainees must be recognized and reflected in the remuneration structures.

INDEX